Slow Down When Someone Dies

By
Lin Carruthers and Kate Clark

"Embrace death and make it your friend – it will guide you."
Sheila Livingstone

Our experience is that stories and information in this book can take people by surprise and bring up unexpected emotion and regrets, especially if someone has been recently affected by a person's death or has had a difficult experience after someone's death in the past. If this happens to you, we hope you are able to find comfort and peace with it.

Kate's aunty

To sisters, Mary and Shiela.

Contents

Part 3

Appendices

Introduction

This book is for you. We invite you to get yourself a cup of tea, make yourself comfortable and read this story about Kate and her aunty:

"My aunty took her last breath away from home. She had been taken to a care home in a crisis situation several weeks before but wasn't expected to die even though she was in her nineties. I had popped in to visit her, and as soon as I saw her, I noticed the signs that she was about to die. My husband and I sat with her, and it was incredible to watch her take off her glasses, put them on the bedside table and leave her body.

"After we settled, I went home, called the funeral director and asked him to take my aunty back to our house so she could be with us. I still remember the funeral director saying, 'Oh, that's not normal, Kate.' It was very normal for me because all my other relatives had died at home and stayed in their beds until they left home for their funeral. Thankfully, when I insisted, he did agree to collect her, and she was back in our home, in bed, within a couple of hours. As it happens, that was the house where she grew up, so it felt completely right. I am so glad I knew that was what I wanted and had the courage to speak up because the days after that were so important to me.

"We knew she had been washed recently before her last breath and didn't feel the need to do it again; it felt more important to leave her in peace on the bed. We didn't know about cooling then, but I don't think it was needed because her cremation was four days later. Like my other relatives who just stayed in bed, there were no smells or anything unusual. The only change I remember noticing was her face becoming sort of translucent, like marble.

"I spent quite a bit of time with her after her last breath. She was in the house, so I was coming and going. It wasn't particularly conscious; it was just natural that I was in and out of her room. But in that time, gradually, day by day, I noticed that I needed to be with her less. I remember standing in the doorway on the third day and realising she had died and that everything was as it should be. Looking back, I feel like we were keeping each other company as though I was getting used to her being dead while she got used to being dead. I felt like there was still a channel between us, which was comforting to me.

"Because my aunty had been in the nursing home, her home carers hadn't seen her for several weeks before her last breath, so we invited them to visit her. They were able to spend time with her privately to say goodbye. We were able to have tea and cake with them and thank them for all the care they had given her because they had been a big part of all our lives for many years while she lived with dementia.

"We asked a funeral director to arrange her cremation and take her to the crematorium, as we didn't know any differently then. Looking back, I think my aunty would have been just as happy being transported in our van. I also asked the funeral director for an eco coffin, and he told me the ones he used were as eco-friendly as any others. 'Okay,' I said meekly, so she was cremated in a traditional, veneered, chipboard coffin. We had a lot to learn.

"Four days after her last breath, my aunty left home for the last time, crossing the threshold she had crossed so many times before. She had a private cremation at her request. My husband and I went to the crematorium and sat silently in the crematorium chapel. We then invited her close neighbours and carers to attend the committal of her ashes to her grave the next day. That felt important, as they had all cared so much for her in her final years.

"I feel like those final days I spent with my aunty gave me time to truly register her death and to register that she had gone in a physical sense."

It is not surprising if the idea of slowing down when someone dies is an unusual one to you. The value of what can be experienced during the days immediately after someone dies is generally given little consideration in our culture. Usually, a short time after someone's last breath, a decision is made to contact a funeral director, and this is encouraged by doctors and nurses. All focus turns to planning the burial or cremation and getting through it. For us, doing this misses an opportunity to fully experience what is happening, and this can have long-term consequences for how we grieve.

One minute, a person is breathing, and the next minute, they are not. This is a tremendous change, but slowing down and being actively involved in the process of releasing someone's body can help us to adapt to that change. Seeing the face change colour, hearing the stillness and touching the cold skin helps our brains to register what has happened and begin to adjust to it. After all, when a pet dies, the advice is to keep them at home until their animal friends naturally stop paying attention to them, usually after a day or so. They look, touch, go away and come back again until they do not need to anymore. They are noticing the physical change that has occurred and taking in what has happened.

In the 1960s, the National Childbirth Trust (NCT) grew from concerns that the natural process of childbirth was being taken over by professionals. The NCT, among others, sought to inform, educate and empower parents regarding childbirth. Similarly, in our minds, there are parallels with the predominance of professional involvement after someone's last breath, which can lead to a disconnection from the natural flow of life. Currently, most people who die in Scotland lie in a funeral director's premises rather than at home, but until recently, it was unusual for people to be taken away to an unfamiliar place with unfamiliar people immediately after they died and for us to be so disconnected from their death.

So why slow down when someone dies? By slowing down, you give yourself the option to consider taking charge: to tend to someone's body and to make arrangements for their burial or cremation. Like many things in life, there are pros and cons to taking charge yourself. When you know what these are, it gets a lot easier to make the best choices for you and for the people in your life. You have the option to take charge of everything—perhaps with support and encouragement from someone with experience—to combine what you want to do with what a funeral director can do for you or to ask a funeral director to take charge of everything. For many people, it is possible after someone's last breath to have the straightforward, gentle experience that Kate had with her aunty. However, a death brings up difficulties in family relationships more often than we might think. Discussion, compromise and cooperation will likely be needed, whichever option is chosen.

In every case, based on research and the stories people have shared with us, we believe it is best to keep someone's body close for at least a day until the initial shock has started to settle and you are in a better place to make clearer decisions. For a surprising number of people, it is natural instinct to keep someone close for several days after their last breath until they, the relative or friend, is ready to hand the body over. And for those people who do not have this instinct, there are practical, ethical and financial reasons why it can still make sense to take charge of someone's body and arrange their burial or cremation. Trust in the process, whatever happens, and know you can always change your mind.

The Evolution of This Book

Both of us have had very different experiences with death in our lives and share a common passion for making these experiences more helpful and meaningful. Our paths touched many times over the years, and we spoke often of the value of tending to someone at home after their last breath. We were asked to write an online course based on Kate's knowledge and experience of the time between someone's last breath and their burial or cremation. The enthusiasm for the course, the questions it raised and the stories we heard inspired us to make the information more widely available, so we have woven together Kate's knowledge with our experiences with death to write this book.

Kate remembers that, in her thirties, she experienced the death of her uncle and then her mother at home. As was her family tradition, both stayed in their bed from their last breath until leaving home for the last time. Following her experience with her uncle, she became a nurse to support people dying at home. First working in a community hospital and then in people's homes, she saw people from all sorts of backgrounds die in all sorts of circumstances.

"Through nursing, I came to realise that very few people were having the comforting, valuable experiences I'd had with my aunty and other members of my family during the days after their deaths. This inspired me to set up the charity, Pushing Up the Daisies, to inform people of the beauty of keeping someone at home after their last breath and to connect people interested in doing so."

When Lin was in her early thirties, three people who were important to her died in the space of a year: her sister's husband, a friend and her husband's mother. She felt powerless to help her son and daughter, aged nine and seven at the time, deal with the death of their grandmother, and she did not know what to say to her husband. It took her a long time to realise how much these deaths had affected her. Their funerals had done little to help her adjust to what had happened. Over the following decades, she tried to work out how funerals could be better.

"I explored becoming a celebrant and a funeral director, but neither felt right. Later, I investigated whether the design of crematoria could be improved since the public areas have changed very little from when they first came into use over 100 years ago. My research taught me the importance of being physically involved in what happens after someone's last breath—for instance, carrying the coffin or walking with the person to the place where they will be buried or cremated. Eventually, I realised it was not about the funeral; what had been missing for me was spending time with someone after their last breath.

"Then, I saw how my now-adult son and daughter reacted when someone important to them nearly died. I wanted to help them to be prepared for the death of a significant person in their lives, but I had no idea how. I began by writing down what I would like to happen when I die but quickly realised that what I most care about is that my children look after themselves when that happens. But how are they going to do that?

"I started writing them a letter, and it dawned on me that, because they live far away, they might not be there when I die—it might be friends or carers making those decisions instead. So I wrote a letter addressing, 'To whom it may concern, upon my death.' I read out this letter at a Pushing Up the Daisies' event, hosted by Kate, and people attending said they found it helpful. I then brought my passion and writing skills to the work of Pushing Up the Daisies."

About This Book

This book gives you information and ideas to help you decide what matters to you when someone dies. In it, we demystify what happens to someone's body when they die and give you all the information you might need to tend to someone at home, if you wish to. By sharing some of our own stories and the stories others have generously shared with us, we aim to give you the knowledge, confidence and curiosity to follow your instincts. In our experience, there is rich potential for finding wisdom about both life and death during this reflective time, whatever one's beliefs, spiritual or otherwise, and we hope to bring inspiration to our readers.

Here, we share our experience of the simple things you can do to look after yourself and look out for each other when someone dies, with or without the person's body as the focus. There is great potential to create meaningful connections with the people around you as your relationships begin to adjust.

In this book, we address issues that stir emotions for some people, and you may be surprised by your reactions when reading the information and stories contained within these pages. If you do experience an emotional reaction, please be gentle with yourself, get support, give yourself time and continue reading once you are ready.

In the UK, it has been estimated that for every death, on average, four people are strongly affected by it. The information we give is oriented towards situations where at least one close person is around someone when they die. However, we recognise that you may be considering your own death, or that of someone you are supporting, with the prospect that there will be no one close at the time. As you perhaps gain new knowledge and perspectives through reading this book, know that it is still possible to arrange for both body and soul to be cared for as desired. For example, there are a slowly increasing number of end-of-life companions and local organisations that are available to help—see Appendix 1 for more information.

The information on legal and cultural matters in this book relates, specifically, to the laws and customs of Scotland. There are slight differences in the legal situation in other parts of the UK and significant differences in other countries around the world. When a death is unexpected, there are legal procedures which mean that some of our suggestions in this book are not possible. However, much of what we suggest is still feasible and may be particularly valuable in helping people come to terms with the situation.

In Part 1, Some Questions To Ponder, we gently introduce topics that are helpful to explore before making decisions when someone dies. In Part 2, Attending To the Practicalities, we give detailed guidance on taking charge of someone when they die, attending to the paperwork involved and tending to their body. In Part 3, Taking Care of Ourselves, we consider how you can look after yourself and look out for others, and we introduce things you might want to do to support your well-being in the days after someone's death. Some of the content is repeated throughout the sections, as we aim to provide all the information to those readers who wish to dip in and out of relevant chapters rather than reading the book from cover to cover.

Death, like birth, is a transition in the cycle of life, just as sunset and sunrise are in the cycle of the day. Although death is natural and unavoidable, it can turn people's lives upside down, so it is reasonable to avoid thinking about it.

We want you to know that you can still hug someone and speak to them in the days after their last breath and that it can be really comforting to do so. We want you to have the opportunity to hand someone over in your own time, when you know in your bones that something has changed forever, and everything is okay.

Part 1

Some Questions To Ponder

When someone dies, so often the question is, "What do we do now?" or "What is the right thing to do?" There is no one right thing to do, so we invite you to use the questions addressed in the following chapters to explore what is right for you.

For us, death is, in equal measure, ordinary and extraordinary. It is awesome and beautiful in its ordinariness. Yet it is, at the same time, much simpler and much more complex than we usually allow it to be. Death can be unpredictable, and it can disrupt the lives of people connected to the person who has died. It might happen after a long time of knowing it was inevitable, like when someone is living with a terminal illness, or it might come out of the blue.

If someone comes indoors on a cold day and you touch their hand, it might be really cold, but you can feel the underlying warmth of their body even if it is only on their wrist. When you touch the hand of a person who has taken their last breath some hours before, their hand is cold, stone cold, and it is still. Perhaps it is stiff as well. It feels very different from the hand of someone who is alive.

In the last hundred years, developments in medicines and vaccines, along with the UK welfare state, mean more people survive illnesses that used to be fatal or do not get them at all. There have also been considerable improvements in housing, health, education and birth control, which mean that families are smaller, people live longer and, therefore, people have fewer experiences of death.

In the same period of time, access to news and visual media has changed beyond recognition. You may never have seen the actual body of a person who has died, but how many images of death have you seen in your life? Those who are now in their eighties grew up with perhaps a wireless radio in the house and a newsreel film at the cinema once a week. As children, those who are now in their sixties might have had a small, grainy black and white television in the house, with the very formal news shown in the early and late evening. Those now in their fifties might have had a colour television and four channels to watch, but people younger than fifty have grown up with an explosion of channels and other media available.

The news has become more visual, with scenes of violence every day. Film and television dramas have embraced the talents of special effects and makeup artists to depict incredibly graphic violence and gory deaths. Even when an on-screen death is peaceful, it will have been altered for dramatic effect, or perhaps the writers simply have no idea what actually happens when someone takes their last breath. We hear the screen-perfect, final words, uttered as the dying person is held in someone's arms, followed by the perfectly timed eyes rolling back. Perhaps, as a result of this, many people are alarmed or repulsed by the thought of being near a dead body, and the lack of opportunity to have a good experience of being with someone who has died only reinforces their fears.

Fortunately, times change, and so do people. Six years ago, a willow coffin, made by a local woman and displayed in an empty shop unit in a Moray town, caused such an outcry that it had to be removed. Recently, a similar willow coffin, that was displayed on a market stall in a nearby town, caused no evident dismay at all, and demand for a leaflet produced by Pushing Up the Daisies called 'Your Options When Someone Dies' was so high that they quickly ran out.

We understand that there are a host of reasons why

many people are scared of death in our culture, and a common reason is unfamiliarity. Anything new to us can be frightening, and all the more so when alarming stories are our only source of information. Death is often portrayed as a skeleton or a hooded figure with a scythe. Given that, until quite recently, illness, injury and childbirth could often result in a person dying, 'meeting the grim reaper' was an understandable image. So then we began to wonder what would happen if its image was updated. What if the character of Death had a new story and appeared as a teddy bear or a grandmother figure? What if Death was seen as a friend—a kindness—and what if Death could be welcomed?

In the spirit of 'feel the fear and do it anyway', we want to help people find reasons to face death, and perhaps then they will discover it is nothing like they thought.

1

What Happens When Someone Dies?

Let's start by taking a moment to think about our bodies. What on earth are they? Some people understand them as a complex network of cells that enable us to operate in a physical world. Others believe they are primarily a vehicle for the expression of our emotions and a container for our soul or spirit. Could they be a coalescence of galactic energy or a spiritualised substance? How do you understand what a body is?

You may have noticed that we sometimes use phrases like 'the person who has taken their last breath'. Why do we not simply say 'dead'? Although people talk about the 'moment of death', both biological and metaphysical models suggest that death is a process rather than an event. It has been described by Pozhitkov et al. (2017) as 'more like a slow shutdown process and not the simple off-switch many imagine it to be'. The definition of when someone is dead becomes more and more complicated as medical technology develops. A person can be brain-dead, but their body still functions with medical assistance. So is there actually a 'moment of death'? Therefore, we sometimes use the term 'after the last breath', as this is a clear moment of change—the consequences of which we address in the following chapters.

We also prefer to use this phrase because, for us, the person does not immediately cease to be a person upon their death. Now, that may be because, as Kate said of her aunty, "It took her three days to get used to being dead, and it took me three days to get used to her being dead." It takes us time to get used to the idea that the person is no longer alive, and so, in that sense, they are still a person. For people with certain beliefs, it may be more specific than that, and we will touch on this later. Still, it echoes the idea that death is a process rather than an event. For example, in some parts of the world, there are also social deaths. In Mexico, a person has three deaths: when they stop breathing, when they are buried and when no one says their name anymore.

Death is a natural transformation process. In ideal conditions, all the materials in the body, including bones and teeth, are transformed into other matter. This transformational process is an essential part of life. It may be 'the end' for one person, creature or plant, but they provide nourishment and a new beginning for a host of other forms of life, and so the cycle continues. Being aware of this transformational process reminds us of how connected we all are to all forms of life on Earth in a complex tapestry. We are witnessing the beginning of this great transformation by being present with someone when they breathe no more and their heart has stopped beating. If we are able to really be there in the moment, we may be rewarded with a greater depth of understanding of death and, through it, life.

Biologically, when someone dies, the heart stops beating and the lungs stop breathing. Body cells no longer receive blood or oxygen and start to die—brain cells die in about three minutes and muscle cells take several hours, while bone and skin cells take several days. The natural transformation processes begin, caused by bacteria, enzymes and other activities, both internally and externally. However, not all cells start to die straight away. Some cell activity actually increases in the period immediately after someone's last breath. For example, stem cells are most active after death as they attempt to repair themselves for days, and in some cases weeks, after someone's last breath.

Gene transcription—a cellular behaviour associated with stress, immunity, inflammation and cancer—also increases following death (Pozhitkov, et al., 2017).

In terms of physics, our bodies are made up of matter and energy. The first law of thermodynamics says that our energy changes in form but is neither created nor destroyed when we die. Our atoms do not disappear; instead they are repurposed. On a metaphysical level, our bodies are understood as energy systems with, for example, a network of chakras and meridians. So you can see that there are many different ways to understand how our energy bodies change after our last breath.

Have you ever spent time with a person after their last breath or had the opportunity to touch them? If not, you are not alone. Many of us are reaching 40 or 50 years of age and have never spent time with someone who has taken their last breath.

Do you know how you actually feel about the death of a person? Do you have any experience to base it on? Or is it based on what the people you grew up with said and did? Maybe they felt children should be protected from death, when the result of that is to render it unknown and therefore frightening. Were they frightened of death themselves? Did they see it as normal or call it repulsive or disgusting? Could your feelings be based on what you have seen on television news programmes or in drama series or films? These are important questions to explore in understanding the part that death has, or will play, in your life.

As a community and palliative nurse, Kate has been in the presence of many people as they took their last breath. She says, "Awe is the feeling of being in the presence of something vast that transcends our understanding of the world. Could it be that being in the presence of death is good for us? I never feel more alive than when I am sitting next to someone in the hours after they have taken their last breath. That the breath has stopped is awesome, but was the person breathing or being breathed, I often wonder? I am in awe of the silence and the stillness too."

How does that description compare with what you think happens when someone dies?

Many of you might know there is an impulse that makes a rose bud open if you allow it. Is this the same impulse that knows how to bring grace around at the time of death if you permit it? Rose buds have opened before and will continue to do so. Our behaviour, however, can influence how beautiful they are and how much awe we experience from them. Our behaviour can similarly influence how we experience the shift from a person being there to being not there to being still there but different—a reminder, perhaps, of why we came into our body in the first place.

2

What Is Traditional?

Before we explore some possibilities for meaningful connection in the time between someone's last breath and their burial or cremation, let us pause, draw breath and look at how our predecessors have dealt with death as well as what people do now. How did things become as they are now, and how would you like things to be in the future?

One hundred years ago, if someone took their last breath in northern Scotland, we would probably have seen the women tend to the body whilst the men dug the grave. People would have come to the house to pay their respects and then, two or three days after the person took their last breath, the neighbours would come to witness them crossing the threshold for the last time. Then, the men would have carried the person, in their coffin, to the grave and buried them. Whisky would have been consumed along the way, and things might well have become a bit rowdy. No women would have been at the graveside, and no words would have been spoken there. There might well have been no involvement at all by the church or minister. Of course, we would have seen different things happening in the cities, where it was possible to have a person's body cremated. This was a historically valuable option because the cemeteries were nearing full capacity.

Fifty years later, in the early 1970s, we might have seen women at the funeral, which was usually held in a church before proceeding to the cemetery or the crematorium. Or there might have been a brief service in the crematorium, fitted into a twenty-minute slot. Most people knew what was expected in the community they lived in. They knew the prayers and the hymns, and they knew what to wear. Around this time, Lin recalls seeing a funeral cortege in the suburbs of Glasgow, travelling along the main road at no more than walking speed, with the other traffic following along behind. A few years later, she witnessed the funeral of a local woman in Inveraray. As a mark of respect, people living along the route closed their curtains and stood in their doorways as the hearse passed.

Having a person's body at home until their burial or cremation was still quite common in the 70s, often with a wake being held around the person prior to their burial or cremation. In the following decades, it became more and more the norm for a funeral director to be called when someone died and for their body to remain at the funeral director's premises until the day of their funeral.

The practise of holding most funerals in a church, with the minister taking the service and often saying the eulogy, has altered over time. Now, family members or friends often speak at the service, perhaps with a celebrant leading it, or sometimes the family does everything themselves. Funeral services are often held in a crematorium, and crematoria have responded to requests for more time to do this by extending the time allotted for each funeral to take place.

More recently, there has been a move away from sombre funerals where everyone wears black as a mark of respect. Instead, we often hear funerals being referred to as celebrations of life, with those attending sometimes being invited to wear bright colours.

Things continue to change. Where she lives in the north of Scotland, Lin was told that, even ten years ago, when the notice appeared in the undertaker's window, the community knew the funeral would be three days later. Now, the funeral might be a week or more after the person has taken their last breath due to such factors as family travelling from overseas or demand for the small number of funeral times to fit best with a funeral lunch or other social gathering afterwards. The option of direct cremation—when a person's body is taken to the crematorium without a service being held there—has also recently become more popular. On these occasions, there might be a funeral gathering held either before or sometime after the cremation.

If the practises of a particular culture or religion are meaningful to you, then hopefully you will be guided and supported by them, but what if they are not? Living in an increasingly less religious society does not necessarily mean that people do not value the sacred or the spiritual. It is, however, more likely that they have to find their own ways to combine their values and beliefs with what happens in life and death.

Our communities are still the fabric of our lives, but the fabric is more complex and multi-layered when compared to times past. Rather than a familiar practise that everyone knows, there are now many possibilities available to us, with more options for an individual response. This involves being conscious of what matters to you and deciding what really is of value. It means you need to determine what you really want to do. We feel there is a great deal of worth in the quiet, the small, the subtle, the seemingly insignificant, the personal, the unique, the homespun and the homemade at any time but particularly after a person has taken their last breath.

As a result of the enforced Covid-19 pandemic restrictions, funerals were limited to very small numbers of people. Anecdotally, from funeral celebrants, quite a number of people seem to have preferred the intimacy of these gatherings, as they found it a relief not having the pressure of a larger social event.

For others, the restrictions sparked their imagination. The story of what happened when a village postmaster died reached us, and we were touched by the thought that went into marking his death. In other times, his funeral would have been a large gathering in the local church, for he was a popular man, but that was not possible. So, instead, a funeral procession was created, with the hearse being led slowly around the village by several post vans. The word spread, and the people of his community lined the streets and clapped for him as he passed. The person who told us about this felt it was the best possible send-off for the postmaster.

So how does Scottish tradition compare to other parts of the world? Cape Reinga, in the very north of New Zealand where the Tasman Sea meets the Pacific Ocean, is sacred to the Māori. The cultural practises that occur there when someone takes their last breath have been handed down over many generations along with their beliefs about what the soul does once it is free of the body.

Lin has visited Cape Reinga, and she says, "Although you can visit Cape Reinga as a tourist, the sacredness is maintained because there are no cafes or shops at the site, only toilets and drinking water. I had the privilege of visiting there in 2013, and I heard about its importance in Māori culture. Māori believe that when someone takes their last breath, their soul leaves the body and travels from wherever they are in the country northwards up through Aotearoa, which is the Māori name for New Zealand, to Cape Reinga. As the land slopes down to the sea, there is a pōhutakawa tree that is said to be 800 years old. The soul goes to the tree and descends into the underworld by slipping down the roots into the sea—Reinga means underworld.

"The soul then travels underwater to the Three Kings Islands, where it climbs out onto Ohaua, the highest point of the islands. There, it turns and takes a last look back at the land of the living before continuing on to the land of the ancestors, called Hawaiki.

"When I attended a Pushing Up the Daisies course some years ago, a young Māori woman was working as a volunteer in reception. She was so shocked that we were attending a course about how to look after someone after they had died that she phoned her mum in New Zealand, who explained that Pakeha, which means White people, don't do funerals the way Māori do. We were honoured that the young woman came to speak with us about their customs. She told us that the person who has taken their last breath is washed and prepared by the older women. 'I will learn that when I am older,' she said. Then, they are placed in an open coffin in the marae, which is the community house in the village or town.

"They stay there for three days whilst people from the community come and eat the person's favourite food, play the games they liked, sing the songs they sang, tell the stories they told and the men perform a funeral haka. After three days, their body is buried. Meanwhile, their soul makes its way north to Cape Reinga.

"The volunteer's description of the time between a Māori's last breath and their funeral feels good to me. It honours a person who has taken their last breath because they are at the heart of their community for the last time."

3

What Is Legally Possible?

The information on legal matters in this book relates to the laws and customs of Scotland. As we mentioned earlier, there are slight differences in the legal situation in other parts of the UK and significant differences in other countries around the world.

So how much do you know about what is possible during the time between someone's last breath and their burial or cremation? Try this quiz and check your answers at the end of the chapter. The quiz gives good insight into what is legally possible, and it can be an excellent way to start conversations with other people too.

In Scotland, there are relevant general laws relating to deaths and funerals, such as committing a public health nuisance or a neighbour nuisance or causing an offence to public decency. Just as you would not walk down the street naked, you need to cover a dead person's body appropriately while transporting them.

Until recently, there were no specific laws relating to deaths or funerals. However, in 2019, Section 65 of the Burial and Cremation (Scotland) Act 2016 came into force. We will say more about this later.

The Right To Decide How Someone's Body Is Cared For
In Scottish law, no one owns a dead person's body, but the executor or next of kin has the right to decide what to do with it and how it is cared for. This can be particularly

1. If someone dies in a hospice or hospital, the most senior clinician has the authority to decide what happens with their body.	True/False
2. It is legal to take someone who has died in a vehicle, so long as it is a van.	True/False
3. You must tell the police before transporting, in your own vehicle, someone who has died.	True/False
4. Anyone can be buried in their garden.	True/False
5. A death must be registered within eight days.	True/False
6. Someone can legally be kept at home for a maximum of seven days after their last breath.	True/False
7. A bereaved spouse or partner has a legal obligation to arrange a funeral.	True/False
8. It is possible to legally ensure how your funeral will be carried out.	True/False
9. It is possible to legally say who you want to arrange your funeral.	True/False
10. You need a funeral director to make arrangements for cremation.	True/False
11. People must be buried in coffins.	True/False
12. You need permission to scatter ashes.	True/False
13. There is an age limit for the donation of corneas.	True/False
14. You can bury someone at sea yourself.	True/False

relevant if someone dies in hospital and the staff is reluctant to allow you to take the person's body away.

Moving Someone after Their Last Breath

You do not need to inform the police when moving a dead person's body in a vehicle, such as from a hospital to home. We are aware of an instance where hospice staff insisted on this, which caused the family distress.

Body Donation to Science

Your body can be donated to science only if you have completed the relevant paperwork before your last breath. Your options are to donate your body to a medical school, for anatomical examination by medical students, or to donate part of your body, such as your brain, for medical research. If you are considering this option, we suggest you discuss it with those close to you. This option means your body will be taken away very soon after your last breath, so people will not have the chance to spend time with you or to have a funeral with your body. It depends on your, and their, priorities. If you are interested in this option, perhaps you could arrange the necessary paperwork and then guide relatives and friends to decide what's best for them at the time.

Organ and Tissue Donation

To be used for transplant, organs such as the heart, kidneys, liver and lungs need to be removed immediately after death. This is only possible when someone takes their last breath in a hospital.

The tissues that can help another living person are heart valves, tendons, skin and corneas. Almost anyone can be considered for tissue donation, but there are lengthy criteria to meet, which require asking personal and intimate questions. If you want to donate your tissues, consider contacting the transplant service to check if you meet the criteria. Tissue donation would usually involve taking the person's body to a hospital. In some areas, cornea donations can be taken at home. We have no personal experience of anyone's tissues being collected after their last breath, but we understand that about 300 corneal transplants take place each year in Scotland.

Currently, in Scotland, unless you have opted out, your organs and tissue could be taken for donation when you die. Opting out is straightforward and can be done online or by phone. Note that if organs or tissue are donated, there is no particular reason why the person's body cannot come home from the hospital afterwards.

Local Rules and Bylaws

While it may be legal to do things ourselves, crematoria and burial grounds will have local rules and bylaws that need to be followed. For example, a crematorium that is a private business can insist you use a funeral director if you want to have someone cremated there.

Most local authority burial grounds have rules that you must use a coffin although this can be challenged on cultural or religious grounds. Natural burial grounds have rules about hygienic treatment and materials that can be buried.

If you want to do anything different from the usual, check the views of authorities in advance, if possible, whether that is the crematorium, the funeral director, the care home or the hospital, for example.

Burying on Private Land

It is surprisingly straightforward to bury someone on private land; this is your cheapest option. However, it is worth considering the fact that having a grave on a private property could affect the property's value. Also, if the property is sold, you may no longer be able to visit the grave, depending on the grave's position on the land and, possibly, the views of its new owner.

If you do carry out a burial on private land, keep a note with the title deeds recording where and when the burial took place—there is no need to record the information on the title deeds themselves, which is costly to do. It is important to note that if the property is subject to a mortgage, you will need permission from the mortgage company. Also, neighbours could theoretically have redress under the common law of nuisance if the burial caused or causes substantial inconvenience or material damage to their property.

If you wish to bury someone on private land, you need to contact the Scottish Environment Protection Agency for advice. They will provide you with important information, such as the required distance of a grave from water supplies and watercourses. There are no laws about the depth of graves. The Natural Death Centre (2023) is a useful source of information that can provide advice about safe grave digging. You do not need to contact the local authority planning department unless there are more than five graves on the property—this is the threshold for when it becomes a burial ground—or you are erecting a structure that requires planning permission. Be aware that although contacting the local authority is not legally required at the time of writing, this may change in light of recently proposed legislation.

Funeral Arrangements

Many people are surprised to find out that it is not possible to legally enforce wishes about funeral arrangements. The section in a will relating to this is not legally binding, so it is necessary to trust people to carry out your wishes. The Burial and Cremation (Scotland) Act 2016 s65 gives you a legal right to name someone to arrange a funeral and a hierarchy of those who can arrange one if this has not been done. However, if someone has not been named to arrange a funeral, a spouse or partner who has lived with the person who has died for at least six months places above children in the hierarchy. This can be important when partners, spouses and children are not blood relatives or do not agree on the funeral arrangements.

Anyone can be named to arrange a person's funeral. There is no legal form for it—it can be written, for example, in a will or on a signed piece of paper. If someone is named to arrange a funeral, it is important to check with them that they are comfortable doing everything that is wanted and have access to the necessary finances and paperwork.

AFTER THE LAST BREATH QUIZ ANSWERS

1. **If someone dies in a hospice or hospital, the most senior clinician has the authority to decide what happens with their body.**
   It depends. Legally no one owns a dead body, but the next-of-kin or nominated person has the right to decide how it will be cared for. The doctor decides whether to refer the death to the procurator fiscal, which may affect this.

2. **It is legal to take someone who has died in a vehicle, so long as it is a van.**
   False. Someone who has died can be driven in any vehicle so long as it does not cause public offence.

3. **You must tell the police before transporting, in your own vehicle, someone who has died.**
   False.

4. **Anyone can be buried in their garden.**
   True as long as you have the landowner's permission and confirmation from the Scottish Environment Protection Agency that it is a suitable position. It does not need to be on the property's title deeds—just add a note to the title deeds, detailing the position of the grave. You may have to check with your local authority if planning permission is required, for example, for a certain number of graves or if a memorial stone constitutes a change of use.

5. **A death must be registered within eight days.**
   True.

6. **Someone can legally be kept at home for a maximum of seven days after their last breath.**
   False. There is no legal time limit.

7. **A bereaved spouse or partner has a legal obligation to arrange a funeral.**
   False. No one is legally obliged to arrange a funeral, but whoever arranges one is obliged to pay for it. The funeral can often be paid directly from the person's bank account or always from their estate before any other debts are settled. Ultimately, the local authority is responsible and will claim the cost back from the estate if available.

8. **It is possible to legally ensure how your funeral will be carried out.**
   False. You can state how you would like it to be in your will, but this part of a will is not legally binding.

9. **It is possible to legally say who you want to arrange your funeral.**
   True. The Burial and Cremation (Scotland) Act 2016 s65 provides the ability to nominate someone to arrange a funeral and a legal hierarchy of those who can arrange

a funeral if this has not been done. In this hierarchy, a spouse or partner comes above children.

10. You need a funeral director to make arrangements for cremation.

It depends. It is not a legal point, but some private crematoria require it. Local authority crematoria do not require it, and staff can provide information to people wanting to make arrangements themselves.

11. People must be buried in coffins.

Partly true. There is no legal need to use a coffin, but the burial authority can require a coffin to be used on their premises. It is not usually required at a natural burial ground where, for instance, shrouds, sheet or blankets can be used.

12. You need permission to scatter ashes.

It depends. You need permission to scatter ashes on land from the landowner. You do not need permission to scatter ashes at sea.

13. There is an age limit for the donation of corneas.

Partly true. There may be age limits in different regions, which can vary over time depending on the availability and need.

14. You can bury someone at sea yourself.

True, but difficult. You need a license … and a suitable boat! There are rules about the burial location and the design of the coffin. Licensed areas in Scotland are off John o'Groats and Oban.

4

What Do We Notice When Someone Dies?

What is going to happen to the body of a person who has stopped breathing? What might you notice? We find that people have many different ideas about this, some of which are quite dramatic. Now, we want to look at the noticeable physical changes in someone's body after their last breath so that you know what to expect. The changes are due to two distinct causes, and we think it is helpful to separate the two.

First are the changes caused by the blood circulation stopping. When breathing stops, the heart stops, too, so blood and oxygen are no longer circulating around the person's body. You will probably see the underside of their body looking mottled or bruised—this is normal. If their body or, for example, their hands are moved in the first hours, this discolouration usually moves. After a few hours, it becomes fixed wherever it is. The skin on the top of their body will become pale and sometimes develop a waxy appearance.

After the last breath, muscles at first become relaxed, so the body is soft, and limbs are floppy. Internal muscles relax, too, so urine in the bladder, faeces in the bowel and any fluids that may be in the lungs or stomach can be released. Unless someone dies suddenly, they have usually not been eating and drinking for some time, so it is unlikely there will be much body fluid. It is unlikely fluid will come from their lungs unless they were congested before death; for example, due to heart disease.

About 3–6 hours after the last breath, muscles begin to stiffen naturally—this is rigor mortis. Then, muscles will relax again over a couple of days and stay relaxed. Rigor mortis starts in the smaller facial muscles and spreads throughout the body. If this stiffness causes difficulty when handling the person, their joints can be moved by massaging their muscles.

Remember, these are the changes due to blood circulation stopping. The other changes that occur are due to the natural transformation processes starting, when the skin can change colour, sometimes taking on a greenish hue. In rare situations, it can become purple or black. If there is organic matter in the stomach or bowel at the time of death, this will continue to be digested and create gas. The gas can swell the tummy and can cause odour if released, just as in life. Sometimes, due to disease, people might have fluid under their skin before they die, which can form into blisters. It is worth noting that if the person had septicaemia before they took their last breath, this could accelerate the onset of these natural processes.

Discolouration of the body might also be caused by blood-thinning medication, unrelated to the natural transformation processes beginning. Furthermore, if the person's death was caused by a heart attack, their face may be flushed.

Over the following days, the person's eyes will gradually begin to look sunken in their eye sockets, and their eyelids and lips may become dry.

We are aware that some people are afraid of the effects of natural transformation processes, and this might put them off keeping someone at home after their last breath. However, these changes are rarely noticeable straight away, and it is possible to slow their onset significantly by cooling a body as soon as possible after death, particularly around the abdomen. In most situations, it takes several days in Scotland and other areas with a temperate climate for the natural transformation processes to be noticeable in someone's body unless the temperature in the room is too warm.

5

What Happens to Us When Someone Dies?

When someone dies, it is a significant change in the lives of those still breathing, which can have substantial psychological and emotional effects. Looking at how our brains work can give us insight into our response in the first few days.

We are most grateful to psychotherapist Avigail Abarbanel for explaining to us the interpersonal neurobiology (IPNB) framework created by Dr Daniel Siegel in the 1990s, which we use to describe what happens in the brain when a significant change occurs. Using the IPNB framework, the following is what happens in simple terms.

The oldest part of our brain is our reptilian brain—the cerebellum. This part regulates our automatic functions, like our breathing. It facilitates the fight, flight or freeze response when we sense danger and makes our bodies do what they do.

Our limbic brain, or limbic system, is the seat of our feelings and emotions, in common with other mammals. It is hard-wired from an early age and is fear-based, so it is concerned for our safety and survival. It activates our fight, flight or freeze response within our body when danger is near.

Our cortex is the newest part of our brain and is responsible for all our higher human functions, such as high-level information processing, language, thinking, planning and more. This is the part that other mammals do not have.

The front part of the neocortex—the executive brain—is our prefrontal cortex. It offers us executive functions, such as regulating our bodies, attuning to others, having emotional balance, calming fear, pausing before acting, having insight and empathy, being moral in our thinking and our actions and having more access to intuition.

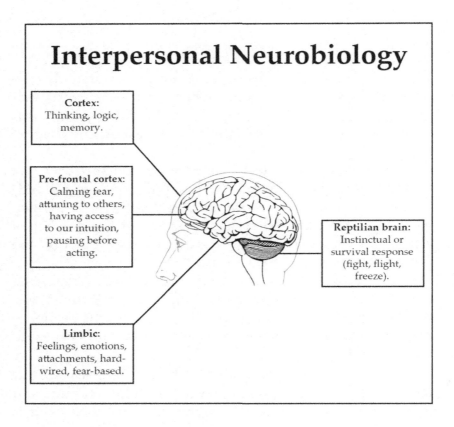

When we feel unsafe, our limbic brain is triggered, and it automatically shuts down our prefrontal cortex unless the limbic system and the prefrontal cortex are well integrated, which in most people they are not. This means that, in a state of fear, we simply do not have access to our higher executive functions such as our ability to modulate fear, experience empathy, retain clear thinking, use intuition, show compassion or sense our meaning and purpose in life. Why is this relevant?

Firstly, the limbic brain tends to have an ingrained fear of dying and a revulsion towards the natural transformation processes of the body. Also, in our current culture, death is unfamiliar to most people, which can make it frightening and feel like a threat to our safety.

Does this help to make sense of someone's reactions at the moment of death? We want to be clear that however someone's brain reacts is the correct and appropriate way for their brain at that time. However, we hope that by considering all we do in this book, it can help you to prepare and integrate your limbic brain so that you can get better access to your higher functions in your prefrontal cortex and have a more meaningful experience. You can do this by breathing, acknowledging your feelings and telling yourself that what you feel is normal and okay. That way, you can be aware of feeling overwhelmed but not taken over by it.

If you would like to learn more, Avigail's booklet, *Grief and Adjustment to Change*, goes into the subject more extensively than we can here.

There is a wide range of reactions to someone's last breath—as many as there are people. Common reactions people have are fear and revulsion and often also, if only momentarily, a feeling of failure because they could not stop it from happening. This illusion, that we could have been in control, can help us feel less out of control. Our limbic system sees death as the ultimate enemy. We naturally feel a duty to keep everyone close to us alive for as long as possible; it does not matter if it is not logical. It is a natural limbic response.

What is important to know here is that people can be surprised by their reactions and may need reassurance that it is okay, for example, to feel relief. People's reactions will also be greatly influenced by their previous experiences

51

of someone taking their last breath. It is important that everyone's needs are met, especially when there is someone present whose reaction is to act immediately and possibly take over. As you will see throughout this book, one of our prime messages is, "Slow down ... there is no rush." In IPNB language, give our limbic brains time to calm down so we can access our ability to think clearly, plan ahead and regulate our fear.

So how do our individual reactions play out when someone takes their last breath? Dealing with death is a tremendous demand on our psychological and emotional resources. As well as dealing with our own limbic brain reactions, we are also often dealing with other people's too—several people are likely to be affected when someone takes their last breath. In addition to those present in the room, others might be on the other side of the world and could be joining in online. It would be unusual if there are no dynamics due to old family stuff: little sisters, big brothers, old disagreements. Family members might not have seen each other for years and, often, for complex and understandable reasons.

There can also be difficult dynamics between people from different areas of a person's life. This can be the case with members of stepfamilies or blended families, particularly if it is the person they have in common who has taken their last breath. In addition, there can be complexities related to illness or dying. It can be difficult, tiring and stressful for those who were close to the dying person, and who might have spent a lot of time caring for them, to come together with people, usually family members, who live away.

Many relationships are likely to be adjusting at this time, not just the relationship with the person who has died. There are changes to relationships between relatives, sometimes in the context of a blended family, and there can also be changes in relationships with the person's care network, which refers to the people who came together to care for the person when they were ill. This network could include formal carers, informal carers, friends or neighbours. These days, people can be ill for a long time before they take their last breath. Intimate, close relationships can build up with both formal and informal carers, and family carers can become isolated in their caring role. Carers sometimes give up jobs or relocate in order to dedicate themselves to caring for an ill person. Once the person has died, carers can face a sudden loss of all the relationships they formed within the care network. They may have a big adjustment to make now that this role has been removed. Later, we will look at ways to ease this adjustment process.

So far, we have referred to the dynamics and relationships involving those central to the life of the person who has died. However, we recognise that many others will likely be affected when someone takes their last breath: professional carers, both long- and short-term; distant family, who maybe phoned several times a week; teachers or fellow students of any age; friends who went food shopping or ran other errands; colleagues or customers; the taxi driver, who was employed for the doctor and hospital runs; and neighbours who kept an eye out. The list can potentially be much longer. How do we take care of these people who may be significant strands in the fabric of the life of the person who has died? How do they say goodbye?

Could the person who has taken their last breath still have a valuable role to play? Could having someone's body at home for several days after their last breath, in and amongst the usual and continual flow of life, give the neighbour a chance to say goodbye? Do these things matter?

6

Why Do People Choose To Be with Someone at Home?

Being with someone's body at home after their last breath often offers a gentle release, an easier adjustment and some unique memories. By simply sitting in privacy and comfort, we can gently begin to appreciate that the person's life, our life, and our relationships have changed forever. Gathering with others offers the opportunity for storytelling and sharing thoughts, laughter and tears, which are all helpful elements in the grieving process. People's choices and motivation will be influenced by their personal beliefs, past experiences, community or family culture and finances.

Being able to have someone at home for the initial few days may support the ability to slow down, giving everyone time to catch their breath and feel what is important to them. For some of us, it is important to know where the person is and who is touching them and tending to them. There can be value, too, in having time to sense the changes in the person. Then, you can register that the person has gone and that their soul has left.

Sometimes, the motivation is to meet the wishes of the person who has taken their last breath. Maybe it is to respect their belief that their soul takes three days to leave their body. Maybe it is because they did not want to be alone after death, and it is felt that, if they are kept at home, they are not alone. Maybe they did not want the 'fuss' or expense of going to a funeral home. Maybe it is their family or cultural tradition and what is familiar.

The choice to be with someone for a few days at home does not necessarily have to relate to an interest or need to physically tend to their body. This is a separate choice which is considered below.

Kate mulled over the question of why she would choose to be with someone at home after their last breath:

"It's important to me to take my time getting used to what has happened. When my relatives died, it took several days for me to really get that they had died and that my life had changed forever. In the first couple of days, I'm usually in a level of shock no matter how expected someone's last breath is, so I don't want to be doing much in the world.

"I find it a precious time to ponder what life is about. Of course, we can do that any day, but there is something supportive in the atmosphere around someone's quiet, still body that deepens that for me. I've experienced the energy around at that time as nourishing and comforting … it connects me deeply to life, just by being there.

"Our bodies are of huge value in the world. In my opinion, to say that 'the body is just a shell' is not giving the body its full worth in the experience of being alive. Sitting with people's bodies in the days after their last breath has brought me an understanding of the human body as an amazing, vital, important creature that I marvel at time and again. There's also an extra layer to it for me: it's an opportunity like no other to realise what it is to be alive."

Our literature search into people's views about being with someone after their death produced few results. The research we have found—see the box below—relates to seeing someone after a traumatic death, but it would be reasonable to believe that this would relate similarly to all situations. Based on this research and also stories of regret people have told us, we encourage people to keep the person's body close for at least a day to minimise the possibility of any future regrets unless they are absolutely sure they do not want to be with a person who has died.

Research into Seeing Someone after Their Death:

Some people know that they do not want to see someone after they have died and have no regrets about not doing so.

Some people find it deeply meaningful and helpful to see someone after they have died and do not regret it even if the person's body is badly disfigured. Few people have regrets about doing this.

People who know they do want to see someone after they have died can have deep regrets if they are not able to do so.

People who do not find it helpful in the short term to see someone after they have died can find it helpful in the longer term.

Professionals can interfere when people want to see someone's body by discouraging them from doing so when they judge that seeing a body will be distressing.

(Chapple and Ziebland, 2010, and Mowll, Lobb and Wearing, 2015).

We believe from the stories people tell us that when a person's last breath has happened outside the home, it may be particularly valuable to bring them home for a few days. In many cases, people have been taken to a hospital in a crisis situation, often when a family member or carer has wanted so much to care for them. There has, therefore, not been a conscious home-leaving or healthy release from the caring role. Could it be helpful to bring the person back home? Carers can then have the opportunity to care one last time, and the person can leave when everyone is ready to let them go.

Having someone's body at home also allows children and pets to do what they do: to come and look, perhaps touch the person gently and then go away again; to come back again and look, go away, return after a while and then go away again until they don't come back anymore. As we said earlier, pet owners are advised to keep a pet at home after its last breath until the other pets have gone through this process and leave it alone, knowing their friend has gone.

There are many practical and emotional reasons why people choose to be with someone at home after their death. It may be helpful to consider, in advance, whether any of these reasons could be important to you:

1. Having time to say goodbye to them in private.

2. Knowing how they are being cared for and who is touching and tending to them.

3. Allowing their soul undisturbed time to leave their body.

4. Having time, in peace and quiet, to get used to the idea that they are dead.

5. Having something purposeful to do for them.

6. Taking charge of what happens after their last breath.

7. Feeling their spiritual presence.

8. Allowing children and other family, friends or carers to spend time privately and comfortably with them.

9. Keeping it natural.

10. Gathering in their presence with family and friends to share stories, memories or laughter.

11. Carrying on family traditions.

12. Managing funeral costs.

13. Involving family and friends in arranging the funeral.

14. Handing them over when you are ready.

15. Giving them 'a good send-off' from their own home.

Lin has not experienced being with a relative during the days after their death but reflected, with this new knowledge, on her mum's death.

"I realised that I would like to have spent time with mum's body in her house. Not doing stuff like clearing the house but just being there, chatting with folk who wanted to come, having cups of tea and getting used to not making her a cup. Getting used to her alarm clock not going off at 8 a.m. and to not hearing the squeak as she put her hearing aid back in after changing the battery. Getting used to her not sitting watching the television, playing the piano, emailing on the computer, putting out bird food, feeding the hedgehog, greeting me at the door or kissing me goodnight when I stayed. I would like to have started to get used to her being dead and started to get to know who I was as a person without her in the world. That is why, in the future, I would choose to have someone at home after they have died."

Tending To Someone's Body

Some people find it healing, intimate, sacred or vital to tend to someone significant to them at this time. Others find it too difficult or not possible. It is a personal choice. Tending to someone after their last breath may feel daunting. It can be confronting, too, especially if the person is young or a child, yet tending to them can also be incredibly meaningful and beneficial in your loss. It can be a last loving act.

The initial preparation of someone's body takes about an hour. If you have not done it before, a nurse or carer may be willing to assist you or do it for you, if you prefer. Whether you participate in this or not, as you start to get used to the change in your relationship with a significant person in your life who has died, being close to their body afterwards in a familiar place can be a special and valuable experience.

Speaking just weeks before her own death, Rosemary told us how she felt when her life partner, Alice, died a few years earlier. Rosemary was a fine storyteller, so we give you her story in her own words. If you wish to see and hear Rosemary telling this story herself, it is on the 'Pushing Up the Daisies Scotland' YouTube channel.

"If I hadn't been in such shock, there is so much to do, like going to registrars and everything and me not having a clue about any of it. Which is, you know ... it's just the norm for a lot of people, isn't it? They don't realise what they've got to do, like get up off their backsides, go the next day, do all these official things, sort out it seems like

… a lot. I know it's probably not, but it seems it. And then, of course, I'm just in shock. Plain shock. I never cried … I never did any of that. I just went on with life, and then I thought, Alice is just up the road at the funeral director's. Why isn't she at home? So I said, 'Oh, I want Alice home,' so she came, and we put candles and everything all over. Beautiful. We spent an absolute bomb on candles. Beautiful expensive candles that smelt beautifully, but God, the expense! I collected them afterwards, to be honest, and wrapped them up and gave them to different nieces and nephews that weren't there, you know, just to say, 'This is what we did for Aunty Alice.'

"My family's culture is, you put things in the coffin that they loved dearly, you know, so Alice … I knew immediately what we had to put in Alice's, which was … she had this cheap, little alarm clock she got from Tesco's. It cost £2.50, and everywhere, all over the world, that blasted clock went, no matter where, you know, just in case. 'The clock must go.' It was like a talisman … like having a teddy bear or something you took religiously everywhere, so that went in, and she had to have a pencil … a few pencils, actually, to be honest, and a rubber and her crossword book 'cos she did crosswords every single evening.

"The priest came. Everybody was, you know, piously getting on with blessing Alice, splashing the holy water all over us and Alice. All this, and we're all being pious with our prayers, and the bloody alarm went off. God, you should have seen the laughter! We laughed and laughed. It was wonderful actually. Isn't it humorous? And we had to get the undertaker to come and undo the coffin 'cos we'd pegged her all down, so they had to come and click the thing off. It was endless, going until it stopped. It always did, but she needed one 'cos she was a bit deaf. She needed one that didn't cut off or snooze, just 'ca ca ca ca'.

"It's having those last possible moments you can with

the actual body. You know it's just a shell, but it doesn't matter. That shell's embodied all that you love in life about this person, you know? So it's just lovely to have it, and it's lovely if you want to have a lock of their hair. You know, I think a lot of traditions that people frown on now are really good to get over grief. You know, you can stroke the lock of hair, you can still feel in touch. I know it's silly … you're not in touch, but, in a sense, you are because, you know, we all leave a part of ourselves in everything. Our skin, our everything, isn't it?

"I find it hard to get rid of Alice's dressing gown. It's as scruffy as hell, and it lies there. And some of her clothes, and I smell them and hold them. You know, when she'd just died, it was lovely to have the nightie she'd died in and to keep smelling it, getting her scent back. I know you're trying to get something that you'll never get again, but I think that having bodies at home, you know, is essential for your own health … mental health. It seems awful that they are shoved away out of the family's reach."

7

Is This Only about the Physical Body?

Around the world, there are many traditions which recognise we are made up of more than our human body and that there is an unseen part of us that is eternal in some way. These have served human beings for centuries. We will not discuss the many views about this here, but it is worth considering how your beliefs affect what you do after someone's last breath.

We both believe that some aspect of us continues after death although our beliefs differ. We also know people who believe that there is nothing after death and others who have beliefs in something continuing after death that are different from ours. Since what happens after our last breath is a mystery, we suggest here that some aspect of us continues in some form. If you do not believe this, we hope it will be helpful to you in understanding and comforting people with this belief while they are dying or when people close to them die.

We will call the part of us that continues after our last breath 'the soul'. So after someone takes their last breath, we are relating to their body and to their soul; we talk about 'keeping our body and soul together'. When someone dies, or we experience any other kind of shock, our body and soul can get disconnected. One of the reasons we explore meaningful connections in the following chapters is to move towards this wholeness in the days between a person's death and their burial or cremation.

Some people believe that the soul separates from the body immediately after the last breath. Others believe this process takes time, from three hours to three days or more, depending on how prepared the person was when they were approaching their last breath. We have looked for information about after-death beliefs and could not find any specifically relating to Scotland. We did find some from the US, Canada and the UK as a whole—areas with a similar culture to our own. According to Roper Center (2014) 76% of Americans and 66% of Canadians believe in life after death, with over 40% of Canadians believing we can communicate with the dead. Interestingly, more young Canadians have positive beliefs about life after death than older citizens (Brean, 2018). The only UK data we could find was from a Theos (2008) survey showing that 70% of adults in the UK believe in the human soul and 53% believe in life after death. So, recognising the limits of statistics and the way questions are asked, this data suggests that the majority of people in our culture believe there is some form of life after death.

The predominant religion in Scotland in recent times has been the protestant Christian Church of Scotland. One hundred years ago, nearly 60% of Scots belonged to this religion, which has reduced to about 10% and is now roughly similar to the Roman Catholic Church. The Scottish Household Survey (2020) found that 56% of adults have no religious belonging, and seven out of ten adults aged between 16 and 34 said they did not belong to a religion. Adults aged 60 and over were significantly more likely to belong to the Church of Scotland than any other age group.

In terms of what happens when someone dies, the significance may be that different generations have different approaches to it and different ideas about what happens next. Also, a significant part of the population may have no clear sense of what happens after death. Many cultures have stories about the afterlife and what the person approaching death must do in order to get there. For instance, in the underworld of Greek mythology, Charon, the ferryman, carried souls across the River Styx in his boat. Cerberus, the three-headed dog, guarded the entrance, and Hades ruled the underworld with his wife, Persephone. This mythical map guided the ancient Greeks on their journey after their last breath.

Having a map for navigating any journey can be helpful, and no less so on the journey after death. Do you have a map for your journey after your last breath? If you follow a religious tradition, you will already have one for the journey. There are differences in beliefs around reincarnation but, by definition, these maps all allow for some kind of a soul and an afterlife. Yet where do people with no religious tradition find a map in our increasingly non-religious culture?

Sarah Kerr of the Centre for Sacred Deathcare offers a map based on nature-based spirituality and consciousness, with a newly dead person crossing the river in a boat from the land of the living to the land of the ancestors.

Anthroposophy, which was founded in the early 20th century by Rudolf Steiner, offers a map developed through spiritual science relating to what happens to the soul as it separates from the body and its ongoing relationship with people who are living.

The teachings of Abraham-Hicks (2023) view death as a simple and immediate release of the physical body by the soul or non-physical being.

Exploring such maps and belief systems can help you to work out what you do and don't believe. For now, think about the soul of someone who has just taken their last breath as it separates from their body. How you tend to the soul will be guided by beliefs about the journey the soul is taking—the beliefs of the person journeying as well as those close to them. People who follow a religious or spiritual tradition have processes and rituals to follow at this time.

Buddhists often request that a body is undisturbed for three days after the last breath. Then, for 49 days after someone's last breath, they read texts from *The Tibetan Book of the Dead* to help the person who has died accept and adapt to their death and successfully negotiate the state between death and rebirth—the bardos. They make offerings, carrying on for months and years.

In Judaism, the idea that the soul remains near the body for three days after a person dies is mentioned in the *Talmud Yerushalmi* (Moed Katan, 3:5): 'For three days the soul hovers over the body, thinking it may go back into it, but when it sees that the appearance of the face has changed, it departs.'

In traditional Irish wakes, women washed a body and wrapped it in a sheet. It was important not to shed a tear on the body at this point, as they believed it would disturb the body and soul.

Roman Catholic funerals focus strongly on liturgy to intercede on behalf of the soul and ease the passage to heaven, believing that prayers can speed their passage through Purgatory. Taking a coffin to the church symbolises the return to God, and their funeral prayers commend the soul to God with the words, "Go forth, Christian soul, from this world."

Hindus do not touch the body unless it is essential, and Hindu sons recite shraddha rites yearly to assist reincarnation.

While in some cultures it is important to bury the person as quickly as possible after their last breath, sometimes within 24 hours, in other cultures, the time period of three days is often significant. People speak of it taking three days for the soul to leave the body and that there should be someone with the body throughout this time, often in the form of a vigil. Whether you regard this time as important to those living, to the person who has taken their last breath or to both, in our experience, three days seems to be the length of time needed for people to get used to someone being dead.

There have been happenings reported in the time before

and after someone's last breath that are beyond our everyday experience, but they are reported often enough to be worth mentioning here. In the days and weeks before death, some people have visions of a specific family member, or a close friend, who is already dead. The person is able to see the family member or friend in the room and will talk with them. These experiences are invariably comforting to the person nearing their last breath and very real to them. They are very different from frightening hallucinations.

Charlotte told us this story of when her Irish grandmother was in the last days of her life:

"I was only 17 at the time, and I was very close to my grandma. Every summer holiday, we would spend weeks in the south of Ireland with her, and I even had my bed in her room. We were heartbroken when we heard the news of her terminal cancer, so my dad and I would visit as often as we could from England.

"Then, we got the call from her carers to say she had significantly weakened, so the whole family travelled over to be with her in her home. I remember it was the Easter holidays. For a few days, she was conscious but made little sense to anyone. And then she slipped into a deep sleep. I would sit by her bedside and hold her hand, talking quietly to her about my favourite memories of our time together. Other times, I would say nothing, but I would stroke her hair to let her know I was there.

"After about three days, she suddenly woke up with a big smile, sat up straight in bed and, with all the clarity she once had, announced to us that William—my grandfather, who had died when I was three—had come to take her, so she had to say goodbye. One by one, she said goodbye to us and gave us a kiss. Then, she settled back down, closed her eyes and slipped back into a deep sleep. A few hours later, she died peacefully.

"Whilst I was bereft, it also allowed me some joy to

know she had seemed so happy to be with her beloved husband again, and this had allowed her to die with no fear in her heart. I was able to sit with my grandma for two further days as she lay in her bed, allowing friends and neighbours to say their goodbyes. It was such a healing time for us all before she left her home for the last time on the way to her funeral."

Some people also report noticing scents that are particularly significant to them. A week before he died, Lin's dad suddenly said, "I can smell pipe smoke. St Bruno's pipe smoke. That's what my dad smoked." He had a big smile on his face as he said this. No one in the house smoked, and his father had died when he was nine years old. Such instances of people experiencing connection, or communication, with those who are already dead are subjective and, by their very nature, hard to prove, but the stories people have told us of their experiences and how precious they are to them have encouraged us to speak of them here. Psychiatrist Peter Fenwick has researched this area, which you can learn more about in the book, *The Art of Dying* (2008).

Sue had an experience with her mum, which she kindly agreed to share here. In the last two weeks of her life, Sue's mum lost interest in wanting to get up and go out. Sue's dad asked Sue, a former nurse, to visit for a week to assess her mum, and it seemed to Sue that her mum had turned a corner.

Before this, her mum had been getting up with her father's help and even going out in a wheelchair at times for lunch despite needing oxygen to help her breathe. Now, she was quiet, calm and self-possessed in a way Sue had never experienced her to be before. Her mother, who believed 'It's a great life if you don't weaken!', had overcome many difficulties, especially in early life. One day, while Sue was there, her mum said, "I can't fight this." Sue felt she had gracefully surrendered.

Another day, as they sat at the table, Sue noticed her mother looking at her half-open hand, which was lying palm up on the table. Her mother said, "I feel like someone is holding my hand." Sue found herself saying, "I am sure there *is* someone holding your hand." The incident was then forgotten.

Soon after that, Sue travelled home, instinctively knowing she would not see her mother alive again. Two days later, she woke in the morning with the question, "What would help my mother leave her body?" She remembered that her mother had always loved to dance and did so at any opportunity, so Sue imagined suggesting to her mother that she dance. Within an hour, Sue had a phone call from her father to say her mother had died suddenly. The doctor had thought she might live for another few months.

Sue's dad was bereft and, during a later conversation, said to Sue, "What upsets me most is that I do not know if someone is looking after your mother." She then recalled the incident at the table and was able to recount it, telling him how her mum had felt there was someone there for her, holding her hand. This news reassured him a great deal and gave him peace.

8

How Can We Honour People after Death?

"When someone central to our life takes their last breath, it is worth taking time to consider how to honour them and their body. I think it really does make a positive difference, certainly to the people alive, and, while we can never be sure, I have heard enough evidence to believe we can also help those who have died and our relationship with them."

— **Kate**

We understand 'honouring' to mean relating to someone with respect, with love, with care, with special attention and with appreciation. This is the way we use it in this chapter. By consciously honouring a person and their body, we also honour death. Death is a vital, integral stage in the continuing cycle of life, and being at ease with it allows us to perceive and receive its gifts. By honouring death, we honour what it is to be alive.

As you honour a person who has taken their last breath, you are also honouring the relationship you had with the person. Your beliefs will determine how you choose to honour them, allied with whatever instinctively feels right to you. Some people regard the body as 'just a shell' once a person has taken their last breath but, to us, the body is a miracle—a miracle when alive and a different miracle after the last breath. The body is a recording of all a person's history. It has grown and changed over the years and made possible all that the person has experienced. Their body has been their home and can be honoured as that.

While for some people it may feel important to be involved in doing most of the practical steps of tending to a body, others will prefer that someone with experience carries out these tasks. Closing the eyes and mouth and gently washing the hands and feet with lavender water can be done purely as a practical task. Alternatively, you can take the opportunity to treat it as an honouring experience with forethought and attention. For example, you can take time to appreciate and give thanks for all that the mouth, the eyes, the hands and the feet have done over all the years of that life. You may pause to recall memories and share them together. Of course, if you are not comfortable having intimate physical contact with a person's body, you can still honour their body. You might make a routine of thanksgiving each day, for example, or create a ceremony.

What is the significance of the first three days after someone's last breath? For some people, there can be a sense at this time of someone's soul leaving their body and an awareness that, by actively tending to the person, the person is fully present during this process and perhaps assisting it. Indeed, in several cultures and traditions, people honour a person by staying close to the body, in vigil, for three days after the last breath. Keeping vigil is generally understood to mean maintaining a constant presence beside someone throughout the day and night. It might include silence or, instead, readings from a favourite book or spiritual or religious texts.

These are the words of Nancy Jewel Poer (2002), known as the grandmother of the US home-death movement, about the three-day vigil after the last breath:

"The point of an all day and night vigil (when it is practical and reasonable to do) with readings, poetry, music and prayer, is the creation of a continuous stream of human consciousness and caring; this stream will follow the one who has made the transition. It creates an accompaniment of warmth and spirit truthfulness for the individual adjusting to a new state of existence. Spiritual substance is built up through the natural comings and goings of the family around a death, and through the prayers and readings (which can also take place far away). Such substance can be especially tangible in the proximity of the one who has died. Those on this side are offering up gratitude, love, devotion, human warmth, and the tenderness of human sorrowing in missing the one who has crossed. The expanding soul and spirit gives back vitality and blessing, which can be full of universal wisdom. The spiritual substance in the space between becomes a mutual creation."

9

What Does It Mean To Take Charge?

When someone central to our life takes their last breath, it is an emotional time. Currently, the usual response in Scotland is that we ask a funeral director to deal with the situation for us. They take away the person who has died, give us the choices they are able to offer and organise everything for us.

'Taking charge' is the phrase we use to describe a different response that we believe can more helpfully support our well-being in the long term. This response is a proactive one that may help us to make sense of what has happened and approach death in a more wholesome way. Taking charge does not necessarily mean one person doing everything themselves; a group of people could do it together. There may also be some professionals involved, such as nurses, celebrants or funeral directors—a funeral director is there to serve and assist you, so you may choose to engage them to do everything, or you may choose to use them to do some things and do others yourself. We suggest that if you want to use a funeral director, take the time to work out what is right for you and others around so that you can be clear about your requests. If you do use a funeral director to make funeral arrangements, remember that you still have the option, should you choose, to keep the person at home.

Taking charge yourself means that there is more potential to have an experience that suits you, nourishes you and helps you to make sense of the situation. There are particular moments that are worth paying attention to:

choosing to tend to someone's body; having meaningful get-togethers; handing someone over when you are ready; and crossing the threshold for the last time. As you read this book, you will learn more about what taking charge entails and be able to make an informed choice about whether you want to do this. We include here the key areas to consider in taking charge.

1. Taking Your Time

How you respond in the first hours and days after someone's last breath is important. Someone's death can be a shock, even when it is expected, and when we are in a state of shock, we are not in a position to make good choices. There can be a tendency to do whatever is familiar, and this may not be right for you in the longer term. By taking charge, you give yourself time. By taking your time, you give yourself the opportunity to make conscious choices that are right for you.

Taking charge allows the opportunity to take account of the unique situation and the people and relationships involved, therefore creating a wholesome experience, which is as relevant as possible to everyone concerned. People's priorities can differ greatly, so it can be complex to navigate a path which suits everyone. Everyone will be influenced by family traditions, cultural traditions, spiritual or religious traditions, local traditions, their previous experience, their finances and their personal values. What matters to you?

2. Taking Charge of a Person's Body

For some people, taking charge of someone's body is a priority. It is their primary reason for taking charge of the entire situation, and they are comfortable tending to the body themselves. However, taking charge of a person's body does not mean you have to have physical contact with their body unless you wish to do so. It does mean taking charge of what happens to their body and perhaps making arrangements for others to do physical tasks. You could get help at home or arrange for the person's body to be taken to a funeral director's premises for some of the time. By taking charge of the person's body, you can have more flexibility in the arrangements and timing of the burial or cremation, which is particularly relevant if you are tending to their body at home.

3. Involving Other People

Taking charge of the arrangements for the burial or cremation of someone central to your life can be a valuable and meaningful experience. However, we encourage you to involve other people as much as possible so that you can prioritise resting and spending time with what has happened. It is easy to be distracted from uncomfortable feelings by being busy arranging things in the days between someone's last breath and their burial or cremation. We suggest you listen to your instincts, notice what feels important for you to do and then include close friends, the wider community or a funeral director to do the rest.

If you choose to have a public funeral, think carefully about how much you want to be responsible for and how much you want to be actively involved. These are conscious choices, and it is important to bear in mind that these choices may include not doing something.

When someone asks if there is anything they can do to help, pause, take a moment and see if something comes to mind.

Kate recalls how people helped with her mum's funeral:

"My mum's funeral was a traditional church funeral, all organised by the funeral director because we really didn't know any differently at that time. We went to the village hall for her funeral tea after the service. My mum had been involved with the village hall for a long time, so the women who put on events at the hall arranged her funeral tea for us. It was lovely to spend time there, in a place familiar to our mum and to us. Financially, it was a good option for us too."

It can be easy to lose track of prioritising what is important to you in the days between someone's last breath and their cremation or burial. Therefore, our invitation to you is to take time to think about how your choices will serve you as you start the process of adjusting to the change that has occurred in your life.

Part 2

Attending To the Practicalities

Doing something you have not done before is easier if you know the process, understand the difficulties and have a manual to guide you. This is what we provide here.

In times past, when people were at home after their last breath, local women, who were also often birth midwives, tended to the person's body and wrapped them in a sheet. The local carpenter came to the home with a coffin in which the person lay until their funeral a few days later. It would generally be familiar people who helped you, which is not often the case nowadays.

If there is no one familiar to guide you, and especially if you have not done it before, it is understandable that you might be anxious at the thought of taking charge of someone after their last breath. In this section, you will find the information you need to take charge of, and tend to, someone after their death and arrange their burial or cremation. The practicalities of tending to someone's body are introduced here. The detailed steps, for those who want them, are in the Body Care Manual at the back of the book.

We urge you to think and prepare as much as possible in advance, especially if you are dealing with the death of someone close to you. We also recommend that, if you have not done it before and especially if you have not prepared in advance, you do not try to do too much at the expense of your well-being. Ask for help, if you can, from others in your community or from organisations like Pushing Up the Daisies. You could also seek support from funeral directors.

In this section, we address the main areas of practical

activity involved after someone's last breath, namely tending to the paperwork in order to legally bury or cremate someone, tending to their body and moving them around. We also consider how the days might unfold as you begin to adjust and settle into the situation.

10

During the First Day

We will speak of the situation in a hospital, care home or hospice shortly, but first, we will look in detail at how the first day might unfold at home if you can slow down.

In our view, the first hour or two after someone has taken their last breath is an important time when practicalities can take a backseat because the priority is to pay attention to what has happened. There is often special energy around — take time to sense it. You will never have this opportunity again. People often feel the need to do something or do the right thing. We suggest you concentrate on taking your time and do as little as possible. Sit down, take slow breaths and feel your feet on the ground.

People can feel restless and fidgety in the hours after someone's last breath. We recognise that doing very little can sometimes be a tall order, but do try not to make any significant decisions, like engaging a funeral director. Keep your options open, and this will pass. After a night's sleep, you will be in a better position to make decisions.

As the day progresses, some practicalities must be gently attended to. If you are at home, when you find yourself naturally starting to move about, there are small things you can do. You can do a little more as the first hour becomes the first day.

Whilst it might feel natural to tuck the person in and keep them cosy as you feel them cooling down, we recommend allowing the body to cool down as soon as possible. Remove any duvet or warm bedclothes, and replace them with a sheet or thin covering. If you have frozen cool blocks or even a sealed packet of peas in your freezer, place these onto their tummy and chest as soon as is practical—see the Body Care Manual at the back of the book for more details. Ensure you cool the room, too, so turn off the heating, and shade any sunny windows.

Then, gently attend to the atmosphere—what is needed will depend on the atmosphere before the person's last breath. You will probably want to open windows to let in some fresh air. Perhaps dim the lighting, tidy up around the bed or play soothing and comforting music.

Tending To a Person's Body
At home, wait until a health professional has visited to verify the person's death before moving them from where they took their last breath or removing any medical equipment. If the person is going to be at home for only a day or two, there is no necessity to do anything apart from cool the room. You will probably want to tend to their body in some way, though, even if it is only by placing flowers around.

If you know someone's body is staying at home for a few days, or you are unsure of how long, it is best to tend to the body within 4–6 hours or at least attend to body fluids—again, please refer to the Body Care Manual section.

If you don't want to tend to someone's body, for whatever reason, you need to find someone who can. You may have a friend with caring experience. There may be an organisation in your area, like Pushing Up the Daisies, that could help. If community nurses have been visiting the person prior to them taking their last breath, it has been our experience that they might be willing to wash and dress the person for you, or with you, if that is your wish. If they have been visiting for some time, they will know the person, and this allows them an opportunity to say goodbye too.

Some spiritual traditions believe that no tears should be shed or strong emotions expressed around the body in the first hours after death, as it can disturb the separation process. So you may want to consider keeping emotions out of the room as much as possible. Calmly encourage and reassure the person on their way if this feels appropriate.

Could You Delay Calling a Funeral Director?

Our experience is that calling a funeral director during the first day usually results in a person's body being taken to their premises. The risk is that this could happen before everyone is ready to hand the person over — particularly quiet voices and carers. Financially, too, it is wise to be cautious. Many funeral directors provide a package costing several thousand pounds once you have made a contract even if you decide you wish to take charge of some aspects of the care and arrangements yourself.

Calling a funeral director can also limit the potential for creativity and meaningful connection that can support your longer-term well-being. For these reasons, we advise that you allow the first day to unfold without this intrusion.

In a Hospital, Hospice or Care Home

If you are in a hospital or hospice, the staff will usually tend to the person's body. If possible, consider beforehand if this is what you wish for. If you have made arrangements to take someone home soon after their last breath, and there is no obvious attention needed, you may want to wait and tend to the person's body yourself at home.

In a hospital or hospice, there will be a cool room or mortuary where the person's body can lie for several days, if necessary, whilst you decide whether to take charge of their body yourself or engage a funeral director to do so. In a care home, you will likely need to make that decision almost immediately after the person dies. There is guidance in Chapter 14 on how to move the person to wherever they will lie.

From the stories that people tell us, having someone at home after their last breath may be immensely important when it has happened outside of the home. Government statistics from 2018 showed that three-quarters of people who are expected to die take their last breath in a hospital, hospice or care home. It is usually possible to take someone home within hours of their last breath if this is your wish, in which case the guidance given here is relevant. You may wish to take time to decide what to do, in which case you can adapt the guidance to your situation—the 'First Day' at home may actually be several days after the person's last breath.

During the First Day at Home Summary:

Cool the room.

Cool the person's body and cover it with a light sheet.

Gently attend to the atmosphere.

Consider any attention to the person's body that is needed.

Calmly encourage the person on their way.

11

Completing the Paperwork

The information on legal matters in this chapter relates to the laws and customs of Scotland. There are slight differences in the legal situation in other parts of the UK and significant differences in other countries around the world.

The paperwork requiring the most attention from you is the death registration and the burial or cremation forms. The information for these can be gathered ahead of time, and the burial and cremation forms can be substantially completed in advance. Free help is often available to complete the paperwork from registrars, burial and cremation authorities and organisations like Pushing Up the Daisies.

The First Step
If someone takes their last breath at home, you first need to contact the GP or out-of-hours service to arrange Verification of Death. This does not have to be done immediately, and there can be a benefit in waiting for a while before you do anything.

As we've said before, you must wait until a health professional has visited before you move the person or remove any medical equipment. However, you can close their eyes, close their mouth and, if necessary, replace a continence pad.

If the person is in hospital, the hospital staff will carry out Verification of Death.

Summary of Paperwork Process

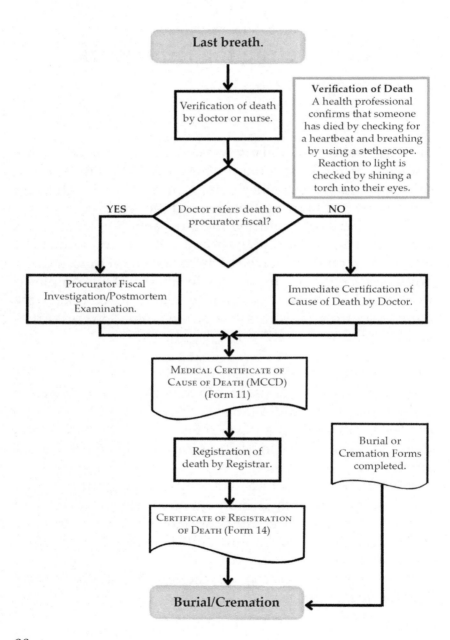

Last breath.

Verification of death by doctor or nurse.

Verification of Death
A health professional confirms that someone has died by checking for a heartbeat and breathing by using a stethoscope. Reaction to light is checked by shining a torch into their eyes.

Doctor refers death to procurator fiscal?

YES

NO

Procurator Fiscal Investigation/Postmortem Examination.

Immediate Certification of Cause of Death by Doctor.

MEDICAL CERTIFICATE OF CAUSE OF DEATH (MCCD) (Form 11)

Registration of death by Registrar.

Burial or Cremation Forms completed.

CERTIFICATE OF REGISTRATION OF DEATH (Form 14)

Burial/Cremation

Medical Certification of the Cause of Death

A GP or hospital doctor will issue a Medical Certificate of Cause of Death (MCCD) soon after Verification of Death if a death is expected and no legal circumstances prevent it. It won't usually be issued immediately, as they need to check medical notes—it would usually be presented to you within 24 hours.

If a death is unexpected, or there are any legal circumstances requiring it, for instance if the person suffered from an industrial or notifiable disease, then the doctor needs to refer to the procurator fiscal—see Chapter 12. If a person has a known life-limiting illness and the death is unexpected, then a discussion between the doctor and the procurator fiscal may satisfy the procurator fiscal that the death is due to natural causes, and this will result in the doctor issuing the MCCD. Otherwise, the procurator fiscal will take charge of the person's body and arrange a post-mortem examination. The pathologist carrying out the post-mortem examination will then issue the MCCD.

Once the MCCD is available, the death can be registered.

Registration of the Death

Legally, a death should be registered within eight days. A close relative usually does this, but other people can do it too—see www.mygov.scot for more information, and follow the link for births, deaths and family. A death can be registered at any local authority registration office by appointment, and it does not need to be done in the area where the death took place. Some offices have longer waiting times than others.

Until recently, you would register the death in person. However, at the time of writing, it is done by phone and email. Once the doctor has confirmed that they have sent the MCCD electronically to the registrar, you can contact the registrar by phone or email to start the death registration process. This takes a couple of phone calls and emails.

Detail of Process Before Registration of Death

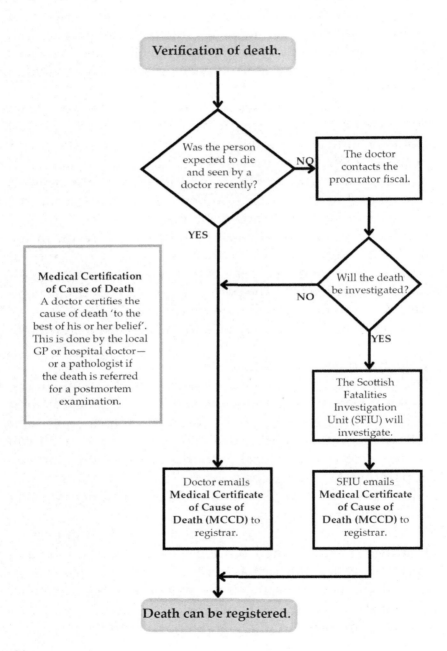

Verification of death.

Was the person expected to die and seen by a doctor recently?

NO → The doctor contacts the procurator fiscal.

YES

Will the death be investigated?

NO →

Medical Certification of Cause of Death
A doctor certifies the cause of death 'to the best of his or her belief'. This is done by the local GP or hospital doctor— or a pathologist if the death is referred for a postmortem examination.

YES

The Scottish Fatalities Investigation Unit (SFIU) will investigate.

Doctor emails **Medical Certificate of Cause of Death (MCCD)** to registrar.

SFIU emails **Medical Certificate of Cause of Death (MCCD)** to registrar.

Death can be registered.

The registrar will provide an abbreviated copy of the register entry for your records. You can buy extra copies to inform banks and other organisations of the death. Most registrars operate a Tell Us Once service to assist with informing government authorities, for example, the pension service—see www.mygov.scot. They will also provide a Certificate of Registration of Death (Form 14) either to you or directly to a funeral director if you use one. This is required for arranging a burial or cremation, which cannot go ahead until 48 hours after submitting Form 14 to the burial or cremation authority.

When you register the death, you will be asked for the occupation of the person who has taken their last breath. We have heard of registrars requiring that it be a paid occupation, but we understand that if you wish to put an unpaid occupation such as mother or homemaker, this should be accepted so long as you are clear and assertive that this is what you wish to do.

MCCD Review and Advance Registration
In the past, two doctors' signatures were required for cremation. Now, only one is needed, but there is a system of randomly selecting about 12% of deaths for review of the MCCD. The registrar will inform you if a review is taking place when you apply to register the death. This review is not an investigation of the person who has died but rather that everything is being recorded correctly. However, it means there could be a delay in registering a person's death of up to three working days, and the burial or cremation cannot go ahead until 48 hours after a death has been registered.

If you have a reason to proceed with the burial or cremation without this delay, you can apply to the registrar for 'advance registration' by completing a short form. If advance registration is given, then Registration of Death can go ahead without delay. Once the Certificate of Registration of Death has been written, there will be no

Detail of Registration of Death Process

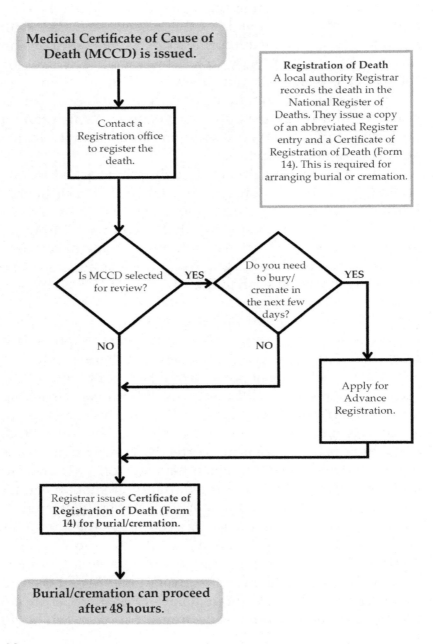

Medical Certificate of Cause of Death (MCCD) is issued.

Registration of Death
A local authority Registrar records the death in the National Register of Deaths. They issue a copy of an abbreviated Register entry and a Certificate of Registration of Death (Form 14). This is required for arranging burial or cremation.

Contact a Registration office to register the death.

Is MCCD selected for review?

YES

Do you need to bury/cremate in the next few days?

YES

NO

NO

Apply for Advance Registration.

Registrar issues **Certificate of Registration of Death (Form 14) for burial/cremation.**

Burial/cremation can proceed after 48 hours.

further investigation.

Cremation and Burial Forms

Each cremation or burial authority will provide its own style of booking forms to give authority to go ahead and also to make the practical arrangements for any service. These can sometimes be downloaded directly from their website. For cremation, you must complete a statutory cremation application form, Form A1, available at www.gov.scot or from a crematorium. These forms can be obtained and largely completed in advance.

Who Can Complete the Paperwork?

Usually, an executor or next of kin would complete the paperwork and make arrangements for a burial or cremation. Recently, it has become legal through the Burial and Cremation (Scotland) Act 2016 s65 to make an 'arrangements on death declaration' to state who an adult wishes to make arrangements for their burial or cremation. The nominated person can be anyone they trust, and it is done by signing a piece of paper stating the wish—there are no legal forms.

If an 'arrangements on death declaration' hasn't been written, the Burial and Cremation (Scotland) Act 2016 s65 gives a hierarchy of those who have the legal right to decide what happens with an adult's body in the case of any disagreement about the proposed arrangements. The hierarchy is the adult's spouse or civil partner, a partner living as if they were married to each other for at least six months, a child, a parent, a brother or sister, a grandparent, a grandchild, an uncle or aunt, a cousin, a niece or nephew and, finally, a long-standing friend. There is a similar relevant hierarchy for a child. The Act says that 'a relationship of the half-blood is to be treated as a relationship of the whole blood' and 'the stepchild of an adult is to be treated as the child of the adult'.

How Long Do Things Take?

It commonly takes a day to get the MCCD from the doctor for an expected death. The time it takes for Registration of Death depends on how long it takes to get an appointment with a registrar. It may be the next day or several days later. The timescale also depends on whether the MCCD is selected for review at registration and whether you apply for advance registration.

For unexpected deaths, additional time may be needed for investigations and a post-mortem examination—see Chapter 12. This may only be a delay of 1–3 days in a straightforward case but can be much longer in a complex case.

The crematorium or burial ground needs their booking forms and Form 14 from the registrar 48 hours before a burial or cremation. So the quickest you can be ready to bury or cremate someone is three or, more realistically, four to five days after their last breath. The actual time it takes to arrange a burial or cremation depends on your choices around a ceremony. For example, arranging a burial or cremation without a ceremony by yourself or through a funeral director will likely be much quicker than arranging a cremation with a ceremony at a crematorium with a funeral director in a prime-time slot.

12

When a Death Is Unexpected

Even when a death is expected, it can be a shock, so when someone takes their last breath unexpectedly, it can be particularly distressing. Not only will you be dealing with the shock, but if the police are involved, you may not be able to see the person or go into the place where they died.

In such situations, the police and other emergency services have procedures to follow which, from your perspective of wanting to be with the person who has died, may not make sense and can feel insensitive to your needs. In most cases, the investigation into the cause of death and the post-mortem examination will delay the person's body being released to you by a few days, but we have heard of occasions when it has taken much longer. At such a time, looking after yourself is particularly important, and much of what we suggest about looking after yourself and looking out for others is still relevant.

When a death is unexpected, the impact of the person's death can be compounded by the distress of not having access to the person's body for some days and also having to deal with the authorities involved. If you can, find someone to support you in communicating with the police, the procurator fiscal and the funeral director appointed by the police to take the person to a place of your choice.

While you are waiting for the person's body to be released, you might want to get together with other people who have been central to the person's life. You might gather photographs or items which were significant to the person and share stories and memories with each other or simply be together if words are overwhelming.

When the procurator fiscal has completed their investigations, they will release the person's body. Their body can be taken home, to another place of your choice or to a funeral director's premises.

Procurator Fiscal Involvement

If a death is sudden, unexpected, suspicious, accidental or unexplained, then the death is referred to the procurator fiscal. This may, but not necessarily, result in a post-mortem examination. Often, if someone has died unexpectedly but with a known life-limiting illness, then a conversation happens between the doctor and procurator fiscal. If it is agreed that the death is due to natural causes, the doctor can issue a Medical Certificate of Cause of Death (MCCD) for registration to go ahead as usual.

If, for any reason, the procurator fiscal decides to investigate the death, the Scottish Fatalities Investigation Unit (SFIU) will do this. In our experience, they are approachable and helpful and can keep you informed of the process. There will likely be a post-mortem examination and also police investigations to determine the cause of death.

Post-Mortem Examination

When the procurator fiscal decides that a post-mortem examination is required to ascertain the cause of death, relatives cannot override this. This may be a full post-mortem or an external examination known as a 'view and grant'. For a 'view and grant' examination, a pathologist examines the body, considers the medical history and the circumstances of death and can certify the cause of death without the need to undertake a full post-mortem examination. However, a full post-mortem examination is required in all suspicious deaths.

Relatives are sometimes asked to identify someone's body at the mortuary before a post-mortem examination is carried out.

Police Involvement

The police have standard procedures for investigating suspicious deaths: homicides, drug-related deaths, suicides and fatal fires. They are governed by law in what they do, which may prevent anyone from either seeing the person for quite some time after their last breath or from entering the place where they died.

When more information is needed to find out the cause of a death which is not suspicious, the procurator fiscal will request a police investigation—this does not indicate that the procurator fiscal regards the matter as criminal. This will involve gathering evidence and interviewing those present at the time of death and others who can provide information. The procurator fiscal will invariably instruct a police report where they anticipate instructing a post-mortem examination.

Medical Certificate of Cause of Death (MCCD)

In all cases, this certificate is needed in order to register a death and proceed with burial or cremation—see Chapter 11. It will be issued either by a doctor following a discussion with the procurator fiscal or, if a post-mortem examination takes place, by the pathologist.

Release of the Body by the Procurator Fiscal

Once a death has been reported to the procurator fiscal, they have legal responsibility for the body, and it will be taken to a police mortuary. In most cases where a post-mortem examination is carried out, the body will be released when the examination is complete, and an MCCD has been issued. In some cases, however, further investigation is needed. When ready, the procurator fiscal issues Form E1 to confirm their release of the body for cremation. It is usual for a funeral director to collect the person's body from the police mortuary and take them to their premises. However, if you wish, it is possible to do that yourself or possibly go along with the funeral director.

More information, and a helpful booklet about the role of the procurator fiscal in investigations of deaths, is available at www.copfs.gov.uk.

13

Key Decisions

We will now look at the key decisions that need to be made, for both expected and unexpected deaths.

Many factors will influence your decisions. As well as family traditions, cultural traditions, spiritual or religious traditions and local traditions of everyone involved, your decisions will be influenced by environmental, personal and other values. Previous experiences, both good and bad, will very likely colour the decisions too. For such a potentially expensive purchase, it would be expected that finances would be a significant influence, but our experience is that this is not the case. People are often willing to go into debt to pay for the arrangements they decide they want.

Your First Decision
Your first decision is usually whether to keep the person who has died in your care, for now at least, or to engage a funeral director to take the person into their care. This decision crucially affects how the following days will unfold. Taking charge and keeping the person in your care alters all the dynamics too. It holds the power in your hands. You are the funeral director.

However, if you choose to use a professional funeral director, always remember that they are there to serve and assist you.

Who Will Take Charge?

Many people do not realise that they have the option to take charge of everything themselves. You could do everything without involving a funeral director, use a funeral director to do some things or use a funeral director to do everything.

Some people take charge of the situation themselves because it can help them begin to adjust to this change in their lives and relationships, and it gives more scope for creativity. They may want to carry out the wishes of the person who has died; they may want to save money, perhaps avoiding going into debt; or it may be that this is what they, or the person's family, have always done.

Others are more comfortable using a funeral director because it is what they expect to do and what their family and friends have always done, and there can be comfort in that familiarity. It could be that they value the service funeral directors offer, or perhaps they don't have the desire, knowledge or time to make the arrangements themselves. More often than not, people do not realise that there is any other option.

Why Choose a Funeral Director?

Funeral directors provide several services: looking after the body of a person who has died; arranging the person's burial or cremation and attending to the paperwork involved; arranging a funeral and supplying a coffin, a trolley—to move the coffin—and vehicles for a funeral.

Funeral directors also routinely carry out hygienic treatment. Hygienic treatment delays the transformation process slightly but is primarily aimed at altering the appearance of the person who has taken their last breath. Chemical liquids are pumped into the body to make the skin look pink and smooth. We believe this process is invasive and rarely necessary. If you are using a funeral director and do not wish for this service, then be clear with them about this. If you decide that it is a priority that someone does not look naturally dead, then you can ask a funeral director to carry out hygienic treatment. This treatment is different from embalming, which gives longer-term preservation using stronger chemicals, for example, for repatriation of a body from another country.

Many funeral directors provide packages and may charge the package price regardless of how much you ask them to do. There is usually an extra callout charge at night and rarely any practical reason not to wait until morning to call a funeral director.

Recently, it has become common for funeral ceremonies to take place several weeks after someone's last breath. This is partly related to people travelling from a distance and also to the limitations on coordinating funeral directors and prime time slots at a crematorium or burial ground. In this case, you will likely want a funeral director to take care of the person's body.

The Natural Death Centre has a helpful handout for using a funeral director. They and the Good Funeral Guide organisation have a recommended list of funeral directors although there are few in Scotland.

Burial or Cremation?
The decision for burial or cremation is often made by the person who has taken their last breath and may be recorded in their will or funeral plan. The options are either cremation in a local authority or private crematorium or burial in a local authority cemetery, a natural burial ground or a private property. Your decision may be influenced by family or religious tradition and financial or environmental considerations. It may also be influenced by availability.

The relative costs of burial and cremation vary with location. The price of burial includes the purchase of a lair—for two or three people—and a charge for preparing the grave for a burial or interment. Cremation is generally the cheaper option and is similar in cost to interment.

It may be relevant to your decision that some private crematoria only accept people from a funeral director for cremation. As far as we know, all local authority crematoria accept people for cremation without one. Some are very helpful. Also, natural burial grounds do not accept bodies that have had hygienic treatment carried out due to ground pollution concerns. Local authority cemeteries do not have this restriction.

Direct Cremation and Direct Burial
Direct burial or, more usually, direct cremation is a service provided by funeral directors, who arrange everything for the burial or cremation as they would usually do but generally without the opportunity to visit the person's body at their premises and always without a public ceremony.

This has become a popular option for people who do not want a funeral service at the same time as burial or cremation. The cost is lower than a traditional funeral and is a good option for those who want to save money or avoid going into debt but do not want to take charge themselves. This can also be a good option when you want to keep someone at home for a few days after their last breath. It gives the freedom and flexibility to focus on what matters to you and those around you. It also gives the opportunity to look after the person who has taken their last breath until you are ready to let them go, without having to be concerned about arranging the practicalities of burial or cremation.

If someone has died in a hospital, and you do not wish for them to come home, it is feasible to arrange the paperwork and take them directly from the hospital mortuary to their burial or cremation yourself. If you wish, you can arrange a separate ceremony, with or without catering at a local place, which has the potential to be a more enjoyable, meaningful and convenient experience without the limitations of crematorium time slots and additional travelling.

Questions to Ask Yourself

To help you think about what might suit you, you could ask yourself the following:

1. Would you be willing to go ahead with a funeral service that could be arranged within a week or less but earlier or later in the day than usual?

2. Would you be willing to have a burial or cremation held separately from an earlier or later funeral ceremony?

3. Would you be willing to hand over the person to a funeral director to wait for a funeral two or three weeks after a person's last breath?

4. Would you be willing to do some or all of the arrangements yourself?

5. Would you be willing to use a funeral director?

Coffins, Shrouds and Other Coverings

Another decision you will make is whether to use a coffin or the alternatives of a shroud, sheet or blanket. This decision will be influenced by the rules of your chosen burial ground or crematorium, the priorities and values of those involved in the decision, your budget and how easy it is to source the items within the required timescale.

A coffin will likely be required for cremation and for burial in a local authority cemetery. People can usually be wrapped in a sheet or blanket in natural burial grounds. On private land, the choice is entirely yours.

To ease moving around, a person's wrapped body can be placed on a board, an old door or something more decorative, such as a willow stretcher. Proprietary shrouds, which have been approved for use in crematoria, are available. However, before buying one, it is essential to check with the crematorium or burial ground you intend to use that it is acceptable. Nowadays, people are not used to seeing someone wrapped in a sheet or shroud, and so it may be wise, if using this option, to advise people attending in advance.

There are many different types of coffins, and it can be difficult to independently source a 'traditional', veneered, chipboard coffin commonly supplied by funeral directors. However, many others are available online. Cardboard coffins are becoming popular, and decorating them is an ideal opportunity for children of all ages, from 2 to 102, to be creative in saying goodbye. We have also seen a traditional, veneered, chipboard coffin decorated with a packet of marker pens and some creativity. Coffins made in Scotland using locally grown willow are available from a social enterprise called Naturally Useful. We have heard that it is now also possible to buy a coffin grown from mycelium, which will break down more quickly than wood to return nutrients to the soil.

Making a wooden coffin can be a labour of love for a woodworker but is not affordable for the average person. A joiner or handyperson could make an inexpensive coffin— for less than £100—out of floorboards or manufactured boards more quickly and easily. Or if you want to make a coffin yourself, the plans for a 'flat-pack' coffin are available from Pushing Up the Daisies. It weighs approximately 50 kg, can be made by an amateur woodworker from readily available materials and can be stored for later use.

The choice of coffin needs to take into account the amount of moving required, the weight of the person's body and whether a trolley, or people who are strong enough, are available to carry the coffin. Wooden coffins are heavier than wicker, cardboard or traditional, veneered, chipboard ones. A shroud or sheet with a rigid board underneath is a lighter option.

Other considerations are how the coffin will be carried, the experience of people carrying the person and the place of rest. Traditional coffins supplied by funeral directors have decorative handles which cannot be used for carrying, so they must be carried on shoulders or on a trolley. Some wicker and cardboard coffins have handles which can be used for carrying. This can be helpful for use by inexperienced people at home. We use a proprietary bamboo shroud with strong handles for moving someone around.

A good point to note, too, is that it can be more difficult, but not impossible, to wash or dress a person in a coffin. By laying them on a sheet inside the coffin, you can use this to lift them in and out of the coffin if necessary. Also, if using a coffin as a place of rest, think carefully about placing it at a height that reduces any barriers to giving a hug or holding a hand.

Funeral Information and Guidance
The Good Funeral Guide (2021) and *The Natural Death Handbook* (2012) provide excellent practical information about arranging a funeral, so we highly recommend them if this is the path you choose. Both books contain helpful information, and the organisations publishing them have excellent websites too.

Kate recalls Jane's story, which illustrates how, once you are clear about the key decisions, it is possible to successfully work with a funeral director to achieve the experience that is right for you:

"Jane's partner, Robert, died at home after a long illness. Jane wanted to take charge of what happened after his last breath, and she tended to his body and wrapped him in a sheet. Robert's wish was to be cremated, so Jane went to the crematorium, and the staff there helped her to complete the forms.

"A friend offered a beautiful place a few miles away that

was perfect for a ceremony to celebrate Robert's life. The convenient day for the ceremony was Friday, but Robert couldn't be taken to the crematorium until the following Monday. However, Jane wanted Robert's home-leaving to be on the way to his ceremony and so was not keen for him to come back home. What could she do? She spoke with a funeral director and arranged for Robert's body to be taken to their premises for the weekend.

"Jane would have been happy not to use a coffin, but it was required by the crematorium, so she bought a veneered, chipboard coffin from the funeral director. Robert's family and friends decorated the coffin with messages and photos during the ceremony, and then Robert went to the funeral director's premises for the weekend. On Monday morning, Jane and a friend drove him in their van to the crematorium and handed him over to the crematorium staff for cremation."

14

Moving Someone's Body Around

Since about three-quarters of people die in a hospital, hospice or care home, you may need to think about how to bring them home soon after their last breath. You have the option of doing this yourself or asking a funeral director to do it for you.

Whether it is feasible to do it yourself depends on the experience, strength and robustness of those involved. It also depends on whether a trolley is available and where you are moving the body to and from. A person's body can be moved whilst wrapped in a sheet on a rigid base or board, but it takes six people to move a 15st/95kg body, so take care of injury risks. It is reasonable for four physically able people to safely move a lighter person.

Asking a funeral director to do it is probably the easiest option, but it is not the cheapest and perhaps not the most helpful for your longer-term well-being. Since it is currently not the norm in Scotland for someone to come home from hospital after their last breath, funeral directors may initially be baffled about you wanting to do it and perhaps unwilling to help. However, our experience is that if you are clear to a funeral director that you want to do something different and are using them for other arrangements, they will very likely be able to help you. Many funeral directors will not help move someone around as a stand-alone service though. Do shop around.

If you are confident about making all other arrangements

yourself but are daunted by, or physically unable to carry out, the task of moving someone around, then perhaps you can get help from within your circle of friends or neighbours. Consider your needs around this and trust your intuition.

Bringing Someone Home

Our main guidance when bringing someone home is to try not to surprise anyone—it could be the first time the staff have been asked about this. If the doctor has no reason to refer a person's death to the procurator fiscal, the next of kin has the authority to decide what happens to their body. However, the staff may not know this. Ideally, if you have any time, discuss your plans in advance so that staff will be more ready and able to help. In our experience, staff can be very helpful. For example, they may help with a trolley.

In a hospital, a person's body would usually be taken from the ward to the mortuary and can be collected from there. If you feel strongly that you would like to accompany the person's body from the hospital ward to the mortuary, then we suggest preparing staff well in advance. We know of distressing disagreements over this as it is not the usual hospital protocol. If it is helpful for you, someone's body could stay in the mortuary until you make the necessary arrangements to move it. A trolley may well be available to move the person's body to a vehicle. In our experience, we have found hospital mortuary staff to be very helpful.

In a hospice, there is usually a cool room where it is possible to spend time with someone's body and where it can be stored, but often, not for so long. You cannot rely on a trolley being available to move the person's body to a vehicle, though, in a hospice.

In care homes, it is likely that the person will need to be moved directly from their room soon after their last breath. However, it is unlikely there will be a trolley available to move the person's body to a vehicle either.

It is worth checking beforehand what equipment is

available to move the person to your vehicle and precisely where you will need to collect the person from. Hospital mortuaries are often tucked away, with no signs to guide you.

If you move a body before it has been decided whether there will be an investigation into the cause of death and before the MCCD is written—see Chapters 11 and 12—then there is a small risk that you could be tampering with police evidence. However, the next of kin has the authority to decide how the body is to be cared for. If you are next of kin and you know that the death is expected, you can choose to move the body before the certificate has been written.

It is worth considering where the person will lie before you bring them home. We consider this later in this chapter.

Moving in a Vehicle

When moving someone in your vehicle, we recommend you cover the person's body with a blanket to avoid causing offence. When moving the person, always bear in mind to keep their head higher than their feet and to place a towel around their neck in case of leakage from their mouth.

Please remember that you do not need to inform the police that you are transporting someone's body. As we have said before, we are aware of incidences where staff have insisted the police are informed, and the resulting confusion has caused upset and distress for relatives. Surprisingly, many vehicles have enough space to transport a person's body. We are aware, too, that the front seat can be temporarily removed from a smaller vehicle to create enough space.

Checklist for Moving Someone in a Vehicle:

The vehicle needs to have enough space for the person to lie flat, allowing space for the coffin, shroud or board you are using.

A cloth or sheet is needed to cover and wrap around the person's body to hold limbs together.

A board, stretcher or coffin is required to keep the body rigid.

Either a trolley or enough physically able people are needed to move the person to and from the vehicle.

The driver must be in a fit mental state to drive safely.

Moving Around the Home

The ease with which someone's body can be moved around a home depends on the number of stairs and corners in the house. It is likely that, if you have not done this before, you may be apprehensive, and this could affect your instincts, which are normally very good allies at times like these. Maybe take some time before you begin to talk through the plan together and discuss any questions people have. Perhaps have a trial run first with the coffin or board loaded with bedlinen.

Certainly, ensure that one person is in charge, especially if you are negotiating corners or stairs. Take your time, and do not rush. Remember that moving the person immediately to the intended place where they will lie is not necessary. They may need to wait temporarily, maybe in a vehicle or hallway, until enough people are available to move them safely. When there is an option, tilt the person's body in the direction to keep their head up—so headfirst upstairs, feet first downstairs.

Finally, consider how you will move their body onto or off the place where they will lie. An extra sheet underneath their body can help with moving them.

Where Will the Person Lie?
Where someone lies will depend on practical factors like the house layout, whether you plan to have a gathering or ceremony with them in the home, and perhaps family, cultural, spiritual or local traditions. At home, the person would usually lie in their own bed, on another bed, on a temporary table or in a coffin. If someone has been ill and sleeping in a hospital bed, you may wish to move them back to their own bed after death and before they leave home for the last time.

If tending to their body, consider the practicalities of washing and turning their body for your safety. Is it in the best position available, for instance, regarding height and access to both sides? If not, it is often possible to tend to someone in a more convenient place, such as the bed where they took their last breath.

If the person is at home before their last breath, consider the room they are in. Might it be challenging to move them out of the house from there after their last breath? If you know you will want to move them yourself with non-professional help, it may be worth considering where they will lie some time before they take their last breath. While they are still mobile, it might be helpful for them to move, if practical, to an accessible ground-floor room.

We have experience of people lying on their own beds,

in a coffin in the living room, in a garden office, in a yurt, in a village hall and in a vehicle.

Lying in a Vehicle

This is currently an unusual option but one worth considering, especially if the layout of the house or the physical capability of the people involved would make it difficult to move someone into the house. When we mention this option, the first thought is usually of temperature. Of course, it is a less feasible option in summer. However, even that is worth considering in a shaded area for short periods and with cooling packs. We have used this option successfully in two recent situations, one where someone came home from the hospital mortuary due to be buried in their own garden two days later and with no easy access to the house. The car was decorated, and LED candles were laid around the body. When it came time for burial, the car could be reversed close to the grave.

Ann's story illustrates how people's wishes can be met, with an open mind, a little forward planning and a vehicle:

"Ann had long promised to try to be with John at the time of his passing and to look after him after his last breath. With Ann's help, he wanted to be buried in a natural setting with a close family gathering. He did not want to use a funeral director. Ann had no experience of any of this but was determined to carry out his wishes.

"In John's last few days, Ann stayed beside him for several days and nights. At the same time, she realised that his passing was imminent and that she needed to be prepared for when he took his last breath and for his aftercare. She researched options for help with John's body, his coffin and his burial. She sourced a willow casket locally and arranged for it to be delivered to the home where John lived. This came with a kind offer from the casket maker, Karen, to help Ann with the care of John's body. Ann found a natural woodland burial ground near to where John had connections in the south of Scotland. The owners of the burial ground reassured Ann that they could provide assistance and equipment for lowering his body into the grave, and they helped her complete the relevant forms. Having talked with them and the family who would be attending, Ann knew that the burial would be able to go ahead soon after John's death was registered.

"John took his last breath as dawn broke, with Ann holding his hand. She was heartbroken, but she knew things had to be done, so she telephoned his close family and the casket supplier. After the doctor had verified his death, Ann sat with John for several hours, listening to the birds, watching the sunrise and quietly talking to him.

"The willow casket arrived, so Ann and Karen gently washed John and dressed him in the outdoor clothes he wanted to wear, including a pair of his father's socks, which Ann had kept safely for John for many years. He was placed in the coffin, and Ann placed treasured photos and objects beside him.

"Ann wanted to look after John until his burial, but her home wasn't suitable, and John had to leave the home soon after his death. This presented Ann with a difficulty since John did not want funeral directors involved. Where could he lie until his death was registered and his burial arranged?

"Over the years, Ann had often taken John out for enjoyable trips in her large van. The solution was that John's casket was placed in her van, where he lay, surrounded with cool packs, which Ann checked and refreshed each day. Once his death was registered, three days later, Ann drove John to the woodland for his burial."

Do I Need a Coffin?

A coffin is not necessary to move someone around. It can make it easier, as people's limbs can be unwieldy. However, wrapping their body in a sheet and lying them on a board can be a practical and appropriate option to address this. The option you choose will depend on a mix of the available suitable alternatives, the rules of any burial or cremation authority you are using and the priorities and values of those around you.

Going to Burial or Cremation

All the above guidance regarding moving the person around is applicable when going to burial or cremation. You will also need to consider what will happen when you get there. The best option will depend very much on who is available to help and whether there will be a ceremony. The crematorium or burial place may have equipment or staff who can assist you. We recommend you discuss your wishes as early as possible with the staff and, once you know what equipment and help are available, discern what is best for you. We have found staff to be very helpful as long as they know your wishes.

15

Before You Begin Tending To Someone's Body

Having considered how tending to someone's body can support our well-being, we will now address the practicalities involved. We hope to demystify the process sufficiently so that you feel confident and can let your intuition help you.

If you have experience with the hands-on, physical care of someone when they were alive, most of the practicalities will be straightforward. However, it may take practise to be at ease with caring for someone after their last breath, so please be gentle with yourself as you learn about it. Whatever you do, remember there is no 'right thing to do'. The information in this book, which includes the Body Care Manual, covers everything you might want to do—you may want to do some of it or none of it.

What matters is that this experience is as beneficial as possible for the central people in the life of the person who has taken their last breath and that this person is honoured to the best of your ability. You can proceed with limited practical care before a person's death has been verified as long as you remember not to move the person's body or remove any medical equipment. If the person who has taken their last breath is going to be at home for only a day or two, there is no necessity to do anything apart from cool the room and, if there is odour, clean up any body fluids just as you would when someone is alive.

Questions to Ask Yourself

We recommend you ask yourself several questions before you begin tending to a person's body:

1. **What are the views of the person who has taken their last breath and all the people concerned?**
   Discuss any of the person's last wishes, and others' wishes and apprehensions, and especially listen to the quiet voices.

2. **Who is going to be present?**
   It may be the first time some people have seen the body of someone who has taken their last breath, and they may need reassurance or gentle encouragement. People can be present in the space without the need to touch or even look at the person's body. However, in our experience, people who are initially fearful or repulsed can benefit even in a small way from taking part in this final act of love.

3. **Who is going to help?**
   For washing and dressing, you will need two able people who are comfortable touching and turning someone. Other people may help in other ways, like fetching things, making tea or just wishing to be present with what you are doing. You may need help from a nurse, doctor or funeral director to remove medical devices, such as a catheter or syringe driver.

4. **Where is the best place to tend to their body?**
   A bed is usually the most practical place, but it is possible to do it in a coffin, if necessary. Consider the bed, or table, position and height to give access to both sides and for safe moving to avoid the risk of injury.

5. Is cooling necessary?

The reason for cooling a person's body is to delay the natural transformation processes, which may lead to odour and noticeable changes in their body. The need for cooling depends on the room temperature, how long the person will be in the home and if particular caution is indicated for any reason relating to their body condition. Pay particular attention to cooling if someone had disease in their tummy area. Tending to the body of a person who is obese, has large wounds or weeping skin or who had septicaemia when alive takes experience. Unless you have such experience, we advise contacting an organisation like Pushing Up the Daisies if you are considering doing this.

Cooling the Body

As we have said, you only need to consider this if you are keeping someone at home for more than a day or two, so it is not always necessary. However, if you are not keen to do this or it will be difficult in some way, seek advice. The aim is to simulate a mortuary fridge, which is easily possible at home. Your options are to cool the body and/or to cool the room. There are advantages and disadvantages to both.

The option we use and recommend is to cool the person's body—see the Body Care Manual at the back of the book for how to do this. You can use several different items: picnic blocks, which you can buy from many supermarkets or hardware shops; gel packs used for physiotherapy; and Cool Cubes. Our local pharmacy has a constant supply of free ice packs in their window. They must come with some medication, so it is worth asking a pharmacist if you want a free supply. Cool Cubes swell up when soaked in water and are then frozen. They stay cool for longer than ice, can be cut into strips and be flexible around a body. Enough Cool Cubes to cool a body would cost around £30.

An alternative would be to hire an air conditioning unit to cool the room, which costs about £150 per week. The main disadvantage we see of this is that it does not cool a body quickly and, because the whole room is cool, it may be uncomfortable for people sitting with the person. The units also make a humming noise, which can be irritating.

In the short term, another alternative, perhaps until you get cooling blocks, is a bag of frozen peas or anything else from the freezer as long as it is sealed. We do not recommend using ice because, no matter how well you think a bag is sealed, the water will usually find a way out when the ice melts.

Body and Tissue Donation
If someone has arranged to offer their body to a medical school or for research into a particular disease, you must contact the relevant organisation as soon as possible after the person's last breath. The organisation will advise what will happen next, and if the person's body is accepted, a funeral director usually arrives within a few hours to collect it.

Organ donation is only possible if someone dies in hospital. If someone dies at home, tissue donation is possible. The person's body would usually, but not always, need to be taken to hospital for tissue donation within 24 hours of the person taking their last breath. If a person is in hospital for organ or tissue donation after their last breath, they can be brought home afterwards.

Pacemakers and Implants
If the person is being cremated, it is essential to know

whether they have a cardiac pacemaker or other potentially explosive devices, radioactive material or other hazardous implants in their body, as they damage the cremator. Once the person's death is registered, you will get Form 14 from the registrar which will tell you whether the person has any of these. You can usually see these just under the skin in the heart area, but be aware there could also be implants in other areas of their body. If a person to be cremated does have other implants, check with the crematorium what their policy is on these.

Metal implants, such as joint replacements, are not a concern.

This is a point of awareness, and you will have time as the days unfold to deal with it. This doesn't have to be addressed before you tend to someone's body, and you only need to think about it if they will be cremated.

What You Might Need

You may consider gathering the things you might need in a special bag, box or basket as someone approaches their last breath, just as you might keep a hospital-ready bag. In addition to practical items, you might want to gather more personal items for the person you are tending to: special soap or lotions; perfume or make-up; favourite or chosen music; or a beautiful scarf to cover their face. You might also want to gather items to tend to the atmosphere of the space where they will lie. You could place beautiful and meaningful items around their body and in the room. LED battery-operated candles can be a helpful and effective alternative to real candles for safety reasons when unattended. You could use this activity as a helpful preparation process in the weeks leading up to someone's last breath.

In addition to gathering practical items, you might walk in nature and pick a leaf from their favourite tree or a stone from a beach you walked along together. Such treasures can be placed on a memory table in their room. You can find a list of the practical items we suggest you gather in the Body Care Manual in this book.

If you are not someone who likes being organised, please do not stress about this. The most important thing we want to highlight here is that most of the items you will need, or their equivalent, will very likely already be in your cupboards. If not, your community nurse may be able to provide some of them. If the person has been in hospital, you could ask the nurses for supplies before leaving.

The things you may not have, and which we would suggest obtaining in advance, are insect mesh for the windows, which you can get online or from hardware stores for about £5, cooling packs if you need them and supportive essential oils or flower essences if they appeal to you.

Supportive Essential Oils and Flower Essences
We find essential oils helpful for several reasons: to slow the natural transformation processes; as an insect repellent; and to create a clear, calming and supportive atmosphere. Lavender is always a good choice because it is antibacterial and also calming for the people around. Frankincense is a sacred oil and is beautifully suited to the situation, too, for its calming properties. Cedarwood is an insect repellent, which can be dripped around the body and on a cloth covering the face.

Flower Essences can also be beneficial for the emotional support they offer at this time. We find Bach Rescue Remedy very helpful. This combination formula helps ease feelings of shock, panic or crisis when we feel we cannot cope. It does this by helping to stabilise our energy system so that we can cope with the intense emotions we are experiencing.

Companion animals are very sensitive to emotions and grieve as we do. You can add essences to their water bowls or food, or have the essences on your hands while you stroke the animal. We include our favourite essential oil blends and more information about flower essences in Appendix 2.

An Understanding of the Difficulties

In our experience, after the initial changes when their blood circulation stops, a person's body usually only changes a little during the first few days after they have taken their last breath. However, it is best to be aware of potential problems in advance so that you can be prepared. Remembering that, in most cases, this is unlikely, it is important to know the situations in which to take extra care. Whether these situations are a problem depends greatly on the attitudes, priorities and experience of the people around you and your access to trusted sources of advice, who can explain what is happening.

Without an experienced, independent person, it can be difficult to navigate the different emotional reactions of the people around so that everyone's needs are met. On the few occasions where we have known a problem, it has been because the natural changes in someone's appearance have caused distress to someone. Bear in mind that these very changes can help us embody, with our senses, the understanding that the person has died. If it is important to keep the person at home, but people feel sensitive about seeing changes in features, skin colour and so on, then covering the body with a sheet or beautiful cover is a good option.

Again, in our experience, changes happen quite slowly, so there is usually time to arrange for professional advice from a funeral director or an organisation like Pushing Up the Daisies. Bodies change after death due to the lack of blood circulation and the natural transformation processes. Since we are as individual in death as we are in life, and whilst there is a typical course of events after someone's last breath, it is not possible to prescribe a one-size-fits-all method. So caution is required in some cases where the natural transformation processes may proceed more rapidly than usual.

As we mentioned before, we do suggest caution when keeping someone's body at home if the person, when alive, is obese, has large wounds or weeping skin, disease in their tummy area or septicaemia. The main noticeable changes indicating caution in the days after someone's last breath would be wounds or blisters leaking fluid, the tummy swelling, skin changing colour or odour from their body. This does not mean you cannot keep someone at home but rather that extra precautions are required.

The main precaution under your control is to slow the natural transformation processes by cooling the body. Where a person is obese, has disease in their tummy area or has septicaemia when alive, we recommend paying particular attention to cooling the body as quickly as possible and keeping it cool. It is also wise to plan not to have the body at home for over a week. Funeral directors have told us that certain medicines can result in a body changing colour quickly or affect the onset of the natural transformation processes. However, we have checked with a trusted pathologist source that this is not the case.

If the person had fragile skin before death, be especially gentle when touching it. Take special care as well to cover wounds under the body and to protect whatever the person is lying on.

While it is necessary to be aware that, very occasionally, things happen unexpectedly, it is important to keep this information in perspective. It would take about 90 days for a body to fully break down in UK summer temperatures and nearly a year in winter. So in the first few days to a week, it is appropriate to expect little activity, in most circumstances, as long as the room is cool. Ensure the central heating in the room is turned off and that the sun is not shining on the person's body, of course.

You will meet Diana again later in the book. She had a fair amount of body fat, and her tummy was swollen due to her abdominal disease. She also had fluid building up under her skin before her last breath. All of these are signs for caution. In the weeks before her last breath, she was given large doses of medication—a reason we have heard a funeral director use to indicate the need to take someone away. However, five days after Diana's last breath, there was no unpleasant odour in the room and no unusual changes in her body. This is within a typical timescale for it to be possible to arrange a burial or cremation.

If you decide to go ahead with tending to a person's body, there is more detailed guidance in the Body Care Manual at the back of this book. Contact organisations like Pushing Up the Daisies for advice if you have questions or concerns.

16

As the Days Unfold

Once the initial shock that someone is no longer breathing is starting to settle, how might the days unfold? Your situation is unique yet may be recognisable to many. Here, we consider the practical activities to be addressed while always bearing in mind the beauty that conscious attention can bring.

If the person's body is at home with you, that will be a strong focus as the days unfold. However, if the person's body is not close by in your situation, much of what we consider here is still relevant to you. If the person is at a funeral director's premises, you can still spend time with their body although this may be limited. Yet they could come home for a home-leaving ceremony. In some areas, there is a tradition of coming home the day or night before the funeral, but it could be at any time that is appropriate or convenient for you.

Your senses can give you valuable information as the days unfold. Just being aware of the stillness of the person who has taken their last breath as well as their pale face and cool skin will tell you, in ways that no words can, that a significant change has taken place. If you feel able to, take time to appreciate them.

At home, small get-togethers with the person's friends and neighbours may occur quite spontaneously. They might be all the more memorable and valuable for that. Perhaps friends and neighbours would like to contribute to a memory table. We explore this more in Chapter 19.

Tending To the Essentials
If you are taking charge of everything yourself, it is important that the paperwork is being arranged—Chapter 11—and that you are sourcing a coffin if using one—Chapter 14— as there are time limitations associated with these. You can allow other activities and details to unfold as people's views and preferences emerge.

We suggest you plan for the cremation or burial within a week if you have the person's body at home. If you are willing to be flexible with the time of burial or cremation, have a separate service or ceremony and arrange everything yourself, then this is usually possible. Unless you are burying the person on private land—in which case you will need to arrange the grave-digging—do check availability with your local crematorium or burial ground before making any other arrangements.

Opting to have the person's body at a funeral director's premises gives you more flexibility with having a person's cremation or burial some weeks ahead.

Tending To the Atmosphere
If the person is at home, you may want to attend to the atmosphere in the room. Be guided by what you know about the person who has taken their last breath, the people around you and what is available. You may want flowers, candles, soft lighting, personal items, a memory table or religious symbols around their body. We also suggest you ensure that plenty of fresh air is in the room for people's comfort.

Tending To the Person's Body
As we have said before, there is no necessity to do anything apart from cool the room if the person is going to be at home for only a day or two. However, you will probably want

to tend to their body in some way, even if only by placing flowers around them.

If the person is going to be at home for more than a day or two, their body needs to be tended to until they leave home for the last time. If close contact does not appeal, then you can get help. We recommend taking steps to cool the body in order to control the natural transformation processes and to control flies. Details of measures you can take are in the Body Care Manual at the back of the book.

People are often concerned there will be an unpleasant odour. Indeed, there is an odour of death, just like birth, which could come from bacterial activity in the body. It could also come from bodily fluids, such as faeces, but this is rarely a problem, especially in people who have died after not eating and drinking for some days. The risk of odour can be minimised by cooling the body and following the guidance in the Body Care Manual. It is possible to keep someone as cold as they would be in a fridge at a funeral director's premises.

Handing Them Over
As the days unfold, you will probably become aware that your need to spend time with the person who has died diminishes. There will come a time, after two days, three days or longer, that you will be ready to hand them over to be cremated, buried or placed in the care of a funeral director. The length of time will be as individual as you are, and there may be considerable variation in readiness within the group of people involved. If possible, wait until everyone is ready to hand the person over because this is a significant moment which we recommend you consciously prepare for. You have had time to fully realise that the person is dead, that something has changed forever, and you are now ready to let them go.

If you are taking the person to burial or cremation yourself, it will naturally happen at your own pace.

However, if you are handing over to a funeral director, they may be eager to help and take things too fast, so prepare them in advance. Think about how, where and when you would like to hand the person over and discuss it with the others involved. Explain your wishes to the funeral directors before they arrive so that they can support and assist you in having a satisfying experience.

Crossing the Threshold

We invite you to consider the significance and symbolism of the person crossing the threshold of their home for the last time. Conscious action while crossing the threshold can acknowledge this one step further from the physical. The person has moved out of their body and is now moving out of their home. Could conscious action at this time also help orient their soul on its journey?

Again, if you are taking the person over the threshold, it will naturally happen at your own pace. If you have tended to someone's body at home and a funeral director is coming to take them to a funeral or to their premises, this can be a time of disruption. We suggest you plan how to manage this. We have known people who have carried the person out of the house themselves and consciously handed them over to the funeral director at their vehicle.

However, just because there is a vehicle does not mean you have to use it. You could consider walking along a driveway or along the road slowly before moving the person's body into a vehicle. Walking together and slowly moving together can be a powerful way of recognising the moment. Would it feel right to have music or singing?

It was common in some areas for neighbours to gather at the gate for the home-leaving. This respects and acknowledges someone's position in the fabric of the neighbourhood too. In some care homes, the staff and residents line up in the hallway to witness the person's final departure.

Now we bring you a story of how one person dealt with the death of her mum and then her dad. It is a story of what is possible with intention, forethought and the knowledge that all is well. It tells of how Pat and Norman Paterson prepared for after their last breaths and how that unfolded. They were happy for their stories to be told and their daughter, Morag, kindly shared her experiences:

"As a family, my mum, Pat, dad, Norman, brother, Alasdair and I have always spoken openly about death and in particular our own deaths, and we have a philosophy that 'life works out'.

"After many active and well-travelled years, Mum and Dad settled in a small coastal town in the north of Scotland, and a year later, I moved to the same town. My parents were now in their late eighties, and my mum was showing signs of dementia, so they were thinking about how and where they might be buried.

"One evening, I went to the community pantomime in the next town. During the interval, I got into conversation with my friend Thérèse. Somehow or other, in a very short space of time, we were talking about natural burials, and both of us were amazed at the synchronicity: Thérèse and her husband Peter farm a croft just outside of the town, and I heard for the first time that they had established and registered burial circles, one for family and one for friends. It so happens that the field leading to the burial ground has been excavated and is recognised as a place of Bronze Age burials, with many stone mounds still sitting amongst the grazing sheep.

"When I told Mum and Dad about it, it was a bit of a WOW moment, and they both felt that life was working out perfectly in response to their asking the question. Within a few days, we all went to visit the croft and crossed the fields to the burial circle on the quad bike. Mum and Dad were able to choose where their grave would be and agreed details of how things would be carried out.

"About a year later, after a lovely lunch that Mum and I had happily prepared together, Mum quietly died during her after-lunch snooze, with Dad—just out of hospital himself—by her side. It was the first time they had been together and alone in months, as I had been living with Mum while Dad was in hospital, and subsequently to help, now that Dad was home. The carers had encouraged me to leave that day so that the two of them could find their way with cooking and living independently. An hour and a half after I left, lovingly waved off by Mum, who was all dressed up as if she was going somewhere, she slipped away.

"Dad, still delicate himself, responded by default. We had agreed what would happen: ideally, die at home peacefully and take it gently and naturally thereafter, culminating in a natural burial. Instead, he phoned 999, struggled to the neighbour's house, an ambulance and doctor arrived and, before I could get there after receiving a phone call, a local funeral director had been called. All the lights were blazing. Everything was super-busy—the opposite of what we had wanted ...

"Dad and I went with things as best we could. We sat for a while with Mum—who was in her chair, wrapped in a cosy throw—calming and quietening the moment with candles and fairy-lights. The funeral director very quietly visited, which I very much appreciated, and agreed they would come a few hours later, which allowed for more sitting-and-being for the two of us, to say goodbye, to massage her hands, to remove her rings, to love her and to talk with and include Alasdair, in Germany.

"In discussion with the funeral director—who looked and talked like my mum's dear brother, we both noticed, which added to the feeling that all was well—we agreed on the simplest of coffins, cardboard, and told of our burial plans at the croft. Mum was kept for a few days at the funeral director's and then, early on the day of the burial, he delivered her in her coffin to the croft.

"Alasdair and I invited only close relations to the burial, which was what Mum had requested, and Dad had agreed with it. The ceremony was very simple: the coffin rode down the field on the back of her grandson's truck, and then family carried the coffin through a glade, with the rest of the gathering following closely after. Dad sat in a wheelchair, at the centre of the group, with hot water bottles on his lap to stay warm. Together with the grandchildren, Alasdair and I lowered Mum's coffin into the ground with straps. We had rose petals to drop into the burial spot, short offerings from myself and Alasdair, a silence for all to remember and be present in their own way, and then the burial spot was in-filled by all the grandchildren, Alasdair and me.

"After that, we went for lunch at our favourite, local seaside restaurant, where my parents were known and loved, and a table had been made available for whatever time we arrived that day. It was as good as it gets.

"In the following year, Thérèse hosted two 'round the kitchen table' gatherings for Pushing Up the Daisies, where friends of hers, who had expressed an interest, could come and find out more about caring for someone after their last breath. I had several conversations with Kate and Lin about what might be possible.

"Just over a year later, after a brief stay in hospital, Dad came home, knowing that he was at the end of his life, and all medication was stopped. Arrangements were made for carers to come in to help, and I was staying at my dad's when he took his last breath at home one evening, a couple of weeks later. Alasdair, too, was there for the last week, and the nearest grandchildren visited on the last day that he was lucid—perfect timing. It was a special, quiet, peace-filled time, full of love.

"Remembering what had happened when my mum

had passed away, and now clearer about what was possible and also more aware of what felt right, I could be more present and deeply listen to life working out. As soon as Dad died, the GP was called to verify the death. The doctor removed the catheter and medication pump and checked that Dad's continence pants were clean and dry—that he was comfortable and free, it felt like to me. I opened the windows to the beautiful, warm evening breeze, lit some candles and intuitively swaddled his head with a white fleece to keep him cosy and nurtured whilst covering his mouth. Alasdair and I sat with him and the peace of the moment.

"Next morning, the community nurse came to collect medications and equipment. I asked if she would help me with my dad and she agreed. She had heard about Pushing Up the Daisies at a palliative care conference and was very happy to help. I was delighted and in awe—it seemed that synchronicity was happening in every moment.

"I cut off the T-shirt Dad was wearing and, with the nurse, eased it away from his body before gently bathing him with essential oils, warm water and a soft cloth. I gently massaged cream on his face and body, feeling an at-oneness with this simple, yet powerfully symbolic, ritual. We checked the continence pants, and since no fluid had exited, we could simply leave them as they were.

"I wanted to wrap Dad in a sheet and, as we were tending to him, I remembered a particular double sheet which Mum and Dad had had all their married life. It was yellow, which is the colour that Buddhists associate with death. My brother and I, together with the nurse, swaddled Dad in the sheet, laying it under him in a kite shape and then folding one point over his feet, another over his head and wrapping the side points around him, creating a beautiful yellow shroud. We placed a sprig of lavender from the garden on his chest. Everything just flowed, effortlessly. I still have a beautiful video of Dad lying swaddled on his bed, with dappled sunlight dancing onto him through leaves.

"When Dad was ready to go, and Alasdair and I were ready to let him go, Peter and Thérèse arrived in their estate car, bringing with them a slightly cut-down door — so it would easily pass through doorways. With the help of a slip-sheet, left by the community nurse for this purpose, we easily slid him from the bed onto the cut-down door, and then the four of us carried his body out to the car. Out of sensitivity to the neighbours, we carried him out of the house covered with a second sheet which, as it happened, had daisies on it. The neighbours from the row of houses all lined up to pay their last respects, which was not planned, it just simply happened, and it was a very moving and special moment. Dad liked to keep things simple, and all of this he would have loved.

"At the croft, Dad was then placed on a trailer, pulled by the same quad bike he and Mum had ridden on when they first visited the site. Alasdair and I walked behind him, past the ancient burial mounds, to the burial circle. With Peter and Thérèse's guidance, we were able to do everything ourselves. It was a new experience for all of us to lower Dad's shrouded body into the grave, and we learned as we went. Mum had been buried in a coffin. It felt very different when we started putting the earth on top of Dad's body without a coffin as we filled in his grave.

"Dad died during Covid restrictions, and it was not possible to have even the smallest of ceremonies, which was, again, ideal and perfect. He didn't want fuss, and he wanted everything to be super-simple. It was. Rather perfectly, the family had already gathered for Mum's funeral not long before, so they knew where the burial spot was, and they could picture the whole process. They had paid respects to both Mum and Dad then. It was enough, and all was well.

"When we had partially filled in the grave, such that

Dad's body was completely covered, plank markers were placed so that his body will be protected if and when the grave is opened up again. Once Alasdair and I had filled in the grave completely—it was shallower this time—we covered it with the stones that had been removed when the grave was first dug for Mum.

"We and our families can go and spend time with Mum and Dad whenever we want, in a beautiful, natural, quiet spot, with their favourite trees and wildflowers around them. It is absolutely perfect … all of it.

"My niece and nephews were in Germany when their grandpa took his last breath. They made little boats, wrote messages to him and floated them out on a lake, along with candles, on the evening of his burial. And so the ripples continue to work out.

"For me, it was very beautiful to be present in the space between Dad's last breath and his natural, simple burial, witnessing his 'landing' in a perfect place for both him and Mum. It felt absolutely glorious to be in this synchronistic flow—which somehow weaved in every detail—and for that, I am so very grateful."

Thank you, Pat, Norman, Alasdair, Morag and all the family.

Part 3

Taking Care of Ourselves

Someone alive and breathing has taken their last breath, so a great change has taken place. Your world will never be the same again. The shock can be disorientating even if their death was expected. It takes time to regain your balance. How can you, and those around you, begin to find your balance again?

So many people, faced with the death of someone significant to them, lose the ability to be clear or assertive about what they want. Only later, and it may be years later, do they realise what they would have liked to have done. It simply did not occur to them at the time because they did not know their options, or they did know them but lost access to that knowledge due to the shock. We look forward to people being offered all their options by the professionals who advise them at that time, be they nurses, doctors, funeral directors or whoever else might be involved. Currently, people are most often advised to call a funeral director because health professionals are also unaware there are other options.

We have heard from people that the removal of someone by a funeral director immediately after their last breath felt like having the person 'ripped away' from them. Just because a practise is common, it does not necessarily mean we are getting it right. To then have unfamiliar people immediately take the person away and leave a void in their place feels, to us, neither gentle nor kind. Caring relationships deserve special attention in this delicate process of tending to, releasing gently and then handing over the person who has died in our own time.

As the days progress, there are simple things that you can do, alone or with others, as it gently comes home to you that this person will breathe no more and that they have left their body. These activities give you opportunities for meaningful connection with each other and with the person who has taken their last breath as you begin to adjust to the changes in these relationships. You may not always be able to have the experience you wish to have, so we will look at ways you can look after yourself when this happens. After a few days, you may begin to feel ready to hand them over for burial or cremation or to a funeral director. When you are ready, you can let them go.

This next story from Kate illustrates the power of the time between someone's last breath and their funeral and how things that happen in that time can be important—not just big things but small things too:

"My friend Joanna cared for her father in the last week of his life. So, too, did her sister. Joanna contacted me during this time because she wanted to keep her father at home for a couple of days after he died. Her sister had been the longer-term carer, and Joanna came to help in the last week of his life. They had different personalities, and the joint caring wasn't easy.

"After their father took his last breath, Joanna wanted to wash his body, but her sister wasn't keen at all. However, Joanna started to wash him, and her sister joined in. Joanna later described it to me as a beautiful, shared experience that will stay with her forever. She and her sister now don't have their father as a connection, so that memory is something that Joanna is very grateful for. And her sister, too, said later that she was thankful they had done it together. Joanna was comforted to have given her love to her father and made the connection with her sister.

"She had a special surprise later that day when a dear aunt, their father's sister, arrived, and out of the blue, she said, 'It gives me hope to see how he has been cared for and that I could be cared for in the same way after I die.' And that has stayed with Joanna. We may never know where our love goes."

17

Looking After Yourself

Someone has taken their last breath. They are still ... completely still and silent. What can you do to experience this as fully as possible?

Your senses can be a great help when taking in what has happened. If the person's body is not at home with you, you might consider spending time with them at the funeral director's premises. The sight of the pale face and still body, the quietness and the touch of cool skin all communicate directly that this person's body has changed. You can gradually become familiar with the changes as the days unfold. If it feels comfortable to do so, you might sit quietly with the person and take time to appreciate how they have changed from when they were alive.

Although it is a widely held belief in our culture that people should not die alone, it is actually common for people to take their last breath when they are on their own, sometimes for only a few minutes. Being aware of this possibility can lead to less chance of disruption in the first moments after someone's last breath.

During the First Hour
The first thing to do at the moment of death, whether at home, in hospital or elsewhere, is as little as possible. There is no rush to do anything. This moment will never happen again.

Many people report changes in the energy or atmosphere

around someone when they take their last breath. It can be a powerful and special experience for the people present, but it is easily dissipated by people coming in who are not sensitive to it; it is a moment you cannot get back. We recommend taking things very slowly around someone's body in the first hour. Some people react to the last breath by wanting to take action, which can be disruptive for others. If possible, divert them away from the body and from calling a doctor or funeral director. We recommend waiting until people have naturally started moving around before calling the GP, as this can break the spell.

During the First Day

By simply sitting in privacy and comfort, you can gently begin to appreciate that the life of the person who has taken their last breath, your life and your relationship with them has changed forever. There is no rush. Everyone will react differently, and all reactions will be the right ones for their brains so should be considered valid. Allow whatever emotions or feelings that come. Remember the limbic brain? You may feel fidgety, but try not to give in too much to that. Could you wait for it to pass?

If you feel able to, direct some attention to your needs and to those of others around you. Does someone want to spend some time alone with the person who has taken their last breath? Notice if you need a rest. Notice if you need physical activity to move energy around. We highly recommend that you take time to rest or to walk in nature if you can. We also recommend that you make no major decisions until after having that rest.

However, we are not saying it is always easy to do this. There can be tumultuous energy around and a twitchy, unsettled atmosphere during the first day. Still, there can be significant benefits in later days if you can get through it without committing to anything.

If you know that someone will not be staying at home,

there is no need to do any body care, but by all means, do what feels right to you. Think about how you could make good use of the time you do have—for instance, by sitting with the person.

When Relationships Are Uncomfortable

Occasionally, people need to face the death of someone significant in their life with whom they have had an uncomfortable relationship. For instance, their relationship might have been abusive or might have broken down, sometimes a long time ago. They may or may not be estranged from the person who has taken their last breath, and other people may or may not be aware of the situation. Also, an uncomfortable relationship with another family member might affect the choices and possibilities open to people.

When this happens, we can do our best to give ourselves permission to be involved in a way that is right for us. Particularly in estranged relationships, there is no need to do anything or be involved in any way if that is what we need. It might be right to make funeral arrangements but not be present at the funeral. It might be right to attend their funeral but take no part in arrangements. No legal obligation exists for anyone to do so in Scotland even if there are no other relatives. In this case, the local authority will arrange burial or cremation and claim the cost back from their estate if available.

Keep in Touch with Your Instincts

You are adjusting to a whole new world, and during the days before the person is buried or cremated, you can take time to be conscious of that. You may have to compromise your wishes with those around you. There may be vulnerable people to take into account. It may be that you have had a similar experience before and are well prepared, or you may be unexpectedly having this experience for the first time. Your instincts are your best allies at this time, so do whatever you need to keep in touch with them. Perhaps you need to rest, go for a walk or have a bath.

Feeling apprehensive the first few times you are in this situation is natural, so make sure the atmosphere around you is as comfortable and supportive as possible for you. If available, use calming essential oils, like lavender, frankincense or Bach Rescue Remedy. Ask for help rather than doing too much yourself if you are responsible for making decisions and arrangements.

Take Time and Allow Things To Develop

The first days can be overwhelming during any major change in your life, like starting a new job or moving to a new house. You don't know where things are or how they work, you are meeting new people and you have to think about every single thing. It is tiring ... or even exhausting. However, as the days progress and you begin to get to know your way around, you start to be able to relax into this new experience.

Because of the likely feeling of being overwhelmed when someone dies, we want to inspire you to take your time making decisions in the first days. After someone's last breath, we understand that this can be challenging, particularly if others are keen to know when the funeral will be or simply to know what will happen next. In these first days, you are adjusting to the shock of a death as well as new experiences and changes in your relationships.

Compare how you respond to an emotional shock with how you respond to a physical injury. If you have been physically hurt, your instinct usually is to hold wherever it hurts and to keep it immobile. You might feel you need to rest it. When someone takes their last breath, whilst there is nothing to show that you have had a major shock and change, you may still need to hold yourself, be still and rest.

Pay Attention To Handing Someone Over

Our experience is that when people are able to stay with the person who has taken their last breath for as long as they need to, there comes a time when they are ready to hand the person over for burial, cremation or to a funeral director. This can be after a few hours but is more often after a few days if no one is putting pressure on them to take the person away.

As we have said before, we encourage you to make a conscious choice to 'hand the person over'. We have learned from people's stories that having a feeling of handing someone over when everyone feels ready has been very important for long-term well-being. Conversely, the feeling of having someone ripped away prematurely has caused long-term distress. When a person's body leaves home for the last time, there is a symbolic echo of the person leaving their body. The person may be leaving home on the day of their last breath, several days after or on their way to the funeral. It is possible to consciously choose to make their home-leaving a meaningful and memorable occasion, as we explored in Chapter 16.

Looking After Yourself on the First Day Summary:

Take your time, and do not rush to do anything.

Wait until people have naturally started to move around before calling the GP.

Try not to call a funeral director straight away.

Encourage people who want to take action to delay contacting a funeral director.

Take time to rest and to walk in nature if possible.

Trust your instincts.

Take time to support yourself, perhaps with essential oils and flower essences.

Use your senses to help you take in what has happened.

18

Looking Out for Each Other

Everyone reacts differently at the moment of death. Some have an immediate need for action, and some are numb. A shock, like a death, tends to polarise things: the chatty get chattier, the quiet get quieter and the busy get busy doing something. The kind of attachment they have, the caring relationship they have, and shock, all affect people's reactions, needs and ability to speak up for themselves. We encourage you to be prepared for this and to be ready to look out for each other.

The research we referred to in Chapter 6 (Chapple and Ziebland, 2010, and Mowll, Lobb and Wearing, 2015) indicates how important it is for their long-term well-being that people who want to see someone's body are able to do this. Also, some people do not want to see someone after their death and have no regrets about not doing so.

So how does this affect how we look out for each other? In our experience, people who have had a caring or intimate relationship tend to want to take time to let go of someone's body. With the best of intentions, others less involved, who want to help, will likely call a funeral director. A funeral director, with the best of intentions, will come 'to take away the burden' and 'to take care of everything' when the burden is a person you deeply want to continue caring for. We have heard many stories from people relating to being unable to keep someone's body close after their last breath. A principal reason for this is that their voices were not heard. We use the term 'quiet voices' to bring attention to this situation.

Even people who are able to speak up about wanting to keep someone's body at home are often unable to do it because the majority want a funeral director to take the body away. If you ever feel that you might want to keep someone's body at home, this is one reason why it is so important to talk about it and prepare the people who are likely to be involved. There are many different 'quiet voices': people who are numb through exhaustion or overwhelmed by feelings; those who have no words to communicate what they need; people who are slow to know what they need or want; people who are shy and not able to speak up; and people who know and say what they need and want but are overruled by others.

These quiet voices often belong to people who have no difficulty making their voice heard in normal circumstances. It could be anyone. It could be you. We have heard from people who have experienced this: how nurses did not hear that they wanted to wash and dress their relative; how funeral directors persuaded them that the person should be taken away when they wanted them to stay at home; how funeral directors dissuaded them from bringing the person home from hospital; and how other people rushed to ask a funeral director to take the person away before they were ready. The need to 'do something now' is the greatest problem facing the quiet voices, who generally need a slower pace.

We want to bring attention to this because we believe that not having their voice heard detrimentally affects people's experience, often unnecessarily, and possibly contributes to more difficult grieving in the long term.

Caring for Carers

We believe it is essential to be aware of the needs of people who have been caring for a person who has taken their last breath. Nowadays, the relationship between a carer and the person they care for can go on, sometimes very intensely and intimately, for many years. If you, or someone you know, is in this situation, it would be worth thinking about what will happen when the person being cared for dies.

Children's nursing policy is written with an expectation that parents will want to care for their child's body after the last breath until they are ready to let go, including, for example, family accommodation often being provided in children's hospices. In adult nursing policy, however, there is no recognition of the need for continuity of the caring role after someone's last breath. Yet after someone's last breath, it is usual for carers, like everyone, to be in a state of shock and find it difficult to think clearly. Additionally, carers may very well be tired because of 24/7 caring or hospital visiting. They may well be the person sitting, numb, by the bedside, possibly overwhelmed by the severing of a strong attachment and the ending of a role that has defined their life.

So what is the best way to look out for carers? Allow a carer to rest before anyone makes decisions about what will happen next. Especially explain the need for this to anyone who, with the best of intentions, needs to be doing something. It is vital to allow time for a carer to start gently releasing the caring relationship and to consider continuing to tend to the person's body for some days until they are ready to hand the person over. It can be the difference between the end of the relationship being a wrench and the carer being ready to let go, and this can have an important impact on their grieving process.

If you are ever in a caring role, or know someone who is, please do consider the importance of releasing this role gradually within the reactions, dynamics and relationships present at the time of someone's last breath. Advance thought and preparation with all the key people around are both very helpful.

A Summary for Carers:

Slow down and do not rush.

Allow time to release the caring relationship gently.

Consider continuing a caring relationship by tending to the body.

At the very least, allow carers time to rest before calling a funeral director—if that is what you intend to do.

Children and young people are also often 'quiet voices'. When we helped a group of Secondary 3 pupils with a project, they all felt that their needs had not been listened to when a close family member had died. The charities Winston's Wish and Child Bereavement UK produce great resources for bereaved children as well as for when a child dies. Child Bereavement UK has created an excellent school resource for developing resilience in children around death and grief. Our interest is in how resilience can be strengthened by what happens in the days immediately after someone's last breath.

We have heard stories of how helpful it has been for young children to keep a sibling's body at home after the sibling has died. They paid attention to it for a few days and seemed to adjust naturally to what had happened. We believe that this applies whenever anyone significant to them has died. Children and young people will spontaneously come up with ways of honouring a person when they are included in what is happening.

It can be tempting to want to protect young people from death. However, we suggest you include young people as much as possible in what is happening. Listen to them, and respond to them. They can be remarkably wise in the face of death.

Looking Out for the Wider Community
How different would it be if the people who were part of the fabric of the person's life came to visit in that first week and spent time with you and the person who has taken their last breath? You might have a cup of tea, a laugh and a cry instead of just a handshake at the funeral. Would that help you to start adjusting to the change that has taken place in the fabric of *your* life? Might it also help them?

19

Creating Meaningful Get-Togethers

During the time between a person's last breath and their burial or cremation, simple intentional activity can connect us with each other and with a person who has died in a new way. From the stories people tell us, we have learned that consciously creating meaningful get-togethers is a helpful way to look after ourselves and each other. A get-together for a shared activity can be a simple way for a group of family members or friends to show love and appreciation and begin to come to terms with a change that has significantly affected them. It allows scope for gentleness, vulnerability, heart connection and new relationships with each other.

Our aim here is to inspire you to consider the benefits of conscious action and to perhaps do things a little differently the next time you are faced with the death of someone central to your life. This can be a creative response to the question, "What do we do?", which can expand to become, "What can we do that would be comforting and nourishing? How do we bring grace to this situation?"

Such shared activities can be simple. They could include sharing memories—it could be that people bring a note, a drawing, a photo or an object that means something to them. These can be put on a memory table, given to the person or put in the coffin with them. People might simply speak words of appreciation. They can do whatever feels appropriate at that time. We might honour the person who has taken their last breath by telling stories of our times together. The language does not need to be complicated. Instead, it is a question of how we process what has happened so that it is real. The important thing, we think, is the bonding, the honouring and the opportunity to say goodbye.

Sarah Kerr, founder of the Centre for Sacred Deathcare in Canada, introduced us to the idea that private, conscious get-togethers can help us to be better ready to benefit from the love and support people offer at a funeral. These get-togethers can help bring home to us what has happened and to experience our feelings. The people involved might only have met in relation to a person's care, and they may never meet again. Still, they share a deep connection with the person who has taken their last breath, and they can benefit from connecting in a meaningful way with each other.

Kate's reflection on Diana's story touches on the benefit of small get-togethers to those who have been closely involved:

"Diana's three good friends had been caring for her 24/7 on a rota for several weeks before her last breath. They were from different parts of Diana's life and weren't close friends themselves. They did a great job of coming together in an intense and intimate situation. A couple of days after Diana's last breath, I realised they hadn't had a chance to say goodbye. When Penny, Diana's daughter, arrived the day before Diana died, the friends had stepped back, so they hadn't seen Diana during her last day or the day after she took her last breath. So I suggested to Penny that she invite them over for a ceremony.

"Penny, her brother, Penny's daughter and the three carers stood around Diana's bed, and all shared a memory of her. Penny told me it was surprising for them because they were memories they didn't all know about. The friends said afterwards what a helpful experience it had been and lovely for her family to hear their stories. It had not only honoured Diana, but it had also honoured her friends' roles as carers. The following week, I went to the funeral, and those three friends were there amongst Diana's other friends. I was glad they had been honoured as her intimate carers. This is something I feel is not done often enough for people who have been close, maybe just before someone's last breath or even quite some time before. These intimate bonding moments help people to pause and to adjust to new relationships."

A special part of Kate's time in the days after her aunty's last breath was when the family invited the carers to spend time with them and her aunty. The carers had been looking after her aunty for many years, and for them to have no opportunity to say goodbye after her aunty's abrupt—and expected to be temporary—move to the care home could have been distressing for them all.

If having someone's body at home is not for you, you can still benefit from these suggestions to make opportunities for meaningful connections with others. Someone's body can be a helpful and powerful focal point, as in the cases of Diana and Kate's aunty, but there are opportunities for meaningful connection without someone's body being present. Examples might be registering the death, eating meals together or gathering where the person lived. There might be a place the person loved where you could gather and do something special together.

It can be particularly helpful to arrange a simple get-together if someone's death is unexpected, when people are waiting for the cause of death to be determined and the person's body to be released.

Preparing a Meaningful Get-Together
When we are arranging a get-together, we find it helpful to take time to think about what we want it to achieve. We call this setting the intention for the get-together. Mull over what you want to do —for example, where you will hold

it and who will be involved, such as carers and particular family members. Consider discussing your thoughts with some or all of the people involved and decide the form it will take. This includes the place, the time and anything you want people to do or bring.

Agree on a few words to express your wish. For example, "We want to share the memory of how we first met Brian and how we will remember him." Or, "We want to honour Sally's carers and thank them for their care." Setting an intention can be likened to drawing back a bow to shoot an arrow that will create a path for the ritual.

There are also things you can do to prepare yourself and to prepare the space. To prepare yourself, you can take time, alone or with others, to set your intention. Cleanse yourself, perhaps by washing your face and hands. Centre yourself, perhaps by meditating or praying. Consciously set thoughts aside to concentrate on the present moment. Concentrate on feeling your feet on the ground and breathing slowly and deeply. To prepare the space, you can tidy and cleanse it, attend to the atmosphere with lighting, music and candles — you could use battery-operated ones if necessary — and bring special or sacred objects.

When you are ready, invite the people involved to focus with words like, "We are gathered here to …" Or you could pray.

Attending the Dying is a small book by Megory Anderson, which we have found helpful as a starting point for ideas on meaningful gatherings related to death and dying.

Small, simple rituals are a great way to include young people and children of all ages in a family's response to a death. Children are great at creating their own rituals, so maybe they could help you to create rituals too. We spoke with a wise young person, all of five years of age, about the time after a person's last breath, and she said, "You could decorate the person [who has died], bake things, do special things, invite special people to parties and watch what happens [to the person who has died]. It's sad, but there are lots of nice things you can do."

20

Preparing for the Days after Our Last Breath

How can we look after ourselves and look out for each other by thinking about our last breath ahead of time and making preparations?

People who put their affairs in order will often plan and perhaps pay for their funeral in advance. It is common for older people to want little fuss and to arrange things so that everything is taken care of. This is a thoughtful approach— it gives those who care for them as little to do as possible— but we invite you to consider whether it best serves those whose lives will continue without them.

What follows are Kate's reflections on Diana's story:

"Diana had a terminal diagnosis. She was a planner and wanted everything in order, including her after-death care, since she didn't want to use a funeral director. Diana had bought her coffin and had designed her funeral service. She'd chosen her celebrant and discussed arrangements with her, and she had even prepared a box with everything that she wanted to be used for the rituals at her funeral service. She had completed her cremation forms as far as she could. She contacted me because she wanted advice about getting from the hospice, where she expected to die, to the crematorium.

"Diana's family lived in Australia and New Zealand, so she didn't expect them to be there when she died but that they would come for her funeral. Her initial plan was that she would be cremated before they arrived, and they would have her ashes at her funeral. In our discussions about Diana's plans, we quickly realised that she still had a role to play in her family after her last breath. Rather than the priority being to 'tidy herself away to the crematorium' and have effectively disappeared when they arrived, it became the priority that she should be an anchor for the family until they did all arrive. So, the new plan was that she would stay at home until they could all be together.

"Shortly after Diana received her terminal diagnosis and was getting organised, she bought her coffin. It had been in her spare room for about six months when she died. In her final weeks, I noticed her body was becoming a bit swollen, so we decided to measure the coffin and discovered it was too narrow. So her friends ordered another one in the same style and sold the original one on eBay. A warning, maybe, not to plan too far in advance."

So Diana thought she was well organised in advance but changed her plans to give her family time with her after her last breath once she learned the value of it.

As you read this book, we hope you will become aware of the possibilities when you take your last breath and the value of discussing them ahead of time. It takes thought and attention to decide what is right for you and to put down in words something that is actually going to convey your wishes. How might you go about it?

We suggest that writing a letter is a thoughtful way to express your wishes to others, and we offer guidance for this later in this chapter. Writing a letter can be helpful to you and give great opportunities for conversations with those who are going to be affected by your death. Sometimes, however, these conversations are not possible for whatever reason, so your letter will always be there when the time comes. You may have to trust that it is of benefit. People knowing that it exists can be helpful in itself, and it might be in your last week that a valuable conversation happens. Remembering what we said about the quiet voices earlier, having a letter to send now to start a conversation could be invaluable when you are no longer able to use your voice.

Talking with Relatives and Friends
Since you are reading this book, you may have been thinking about these matters for a while, whether for your own last breath or someone else's. You might even find yourself enthused about the possibilities it has opened up.

However, most people think very little, if at all, about death. If everyone concerned is in good health, they see no reason to consider it. Even the idea of talking about it may alarm them, which can make them unable to discuss it. So we encourage you to be gentle with them and, if possible, imagine yourself in their position. Imagine how afraid they might be of themselves, or someone they care about, dying. A refusal to talk about it now need not be the end of the discussion, but it might be some time before they are ready to speak with you about it, if ever. Kathryn Mannix's book, *Listen: How to Find the Words for Tender Conversations*, (2021), may help you find gentle ways to talk with your relatives and friends about your wishes.

For you, having someone at home after their last breath may be the best way to honour them and to give yourself the time and space to begin to adjust to their death. For other people, doing things yourself may seem disrespectful, and until they are ready to hear what you have to say, they may not be able to take it in.

For instance, what if it feels important to you that your son or daughter looks after you at home after your last breath, but they say they do not want to? Well, the first thing to do is to pause and not fret. If this is the first time you have raised the subject, there could be a whirlwind of thoughts going around in their head. This is new to them, so they might not be thinking about you being ill or dying. Their

161

wishes matter just as much as yours do, and who knows how things might change between now and your last breath? The situation may be very different when the time comes, and your ideas, or theirs, might have altered. Remember that, in time, relationships and thoughts about being cared for can change depending on circumstances. So be easy on your relatives and friends. Give them time. Notice how you feel, perhaps acknowledging your disappointment, and then consider what matters to you.

In the meantime, be aware that you can do many other things. You might contact an end-of-life companion and speak with them about your wishes and how they might meet them. You can continue to make your preparations as your relatives and friends process your wishes.

Charlotte, who we met earlier with her Irish grandma, spoke of how she raised the subject with her parents:

"My dad will be 80 this year and my mum will be 77, and both of them have suffered from heart problems over the last couple of years. I'm the talker in the family, so they are very used to me broaching sensitive subjects where I wish to find answers. I am also a terrible worrier, so it makes me fret not knowing what their wishes are for after their last breaths. I felt it was time to encourage them to really think about it.

"My dad immediately said he had just about decided that he wanted to be cremated and his ashes scattered around the areas of his childhood homes in the south of Ireland. My grandfather had been a rector, so they had moved between three rectories when my dad was growing up. My mum just looked at him, incredulous, and said, 'What about me?' My dad then answered that he just thought she would be cremated and scattered alongside him. 'But what if I don't want to be scattered in Ireland?' she said. 'What if I want to be scattered in Cumbria, where I grew up? Or here, where we have made a life for ourselves?' My dad seemed quite surprised, as he hadn't thought it through enough at all. And although it came across as quite a comical bickering match between my two fantastic parents, joking aside, it raised my point exactly. If they didn't really have a clue about what they wanted to happen after their last breaths, what chance did I have in ensuring I got it right for both of them, equally?

"I ended that conversation by asking them to really give it some proper thought, otherwise Dad would end up in the celestial equivalent of a dog house for eternity, with Mum grumping at him about her ashes being scattered in the wrong place!"

While approaching the subject face-to-face is one way of preparing people for your last breath, perhaps the letter we spoke about gives the recipient time to take in what you are saying and to begin to consider how they might respond to you. It might make the conversation easier.

Rick's letter is an example of one way of opening up the topic:

Dear All,

I'm not as young as I used to be even if I still felt twenty-five last birthday ... at least inside! So I think it's time we talked about when I'm not here chatting with everyone. At first, I thought I'd sit you all down together when I was in your part of the world, but then I realised it would be unfair to spring it on you, so I decided to write instead, which gives you something to hold onto and refer back to.

Until a few days ago, I'd have said that when I die, I want my body disposed of as quickly and cheaply as possible with no fuss. Now, I'm not sure that would be the best thing for you. What happened to change my mind? I went to a get-together to learn about a charity called Pushing Up the Daisies who, they say, 'support people in looking after a person who has died'. Joy and I have been talking about getting things sorted out before either of us goes, and this seemed an excellent place to start.

There were eleven of us there, two from Pushing Up the Daisies, and the whole session was a right eye-opener. There were practical details about keeping the body cool and making sure flies don't get in, but what got to me was folk talking about their experiences. Some had had what I would call a 'normal' experience—someone died, maybe a parent or a grandparent, and then the funeral director came, took the body away, came by later to talk with the folk and offer them options for coffins, flowers, cars and the like. Did they want burial or cremation? Then the funeral director went off and sorted it out. Everyone turned up for the funeral a week later, and that was that. That's what everyone does, right? Except that three or four folk spoke of having regrets afterwards—they had wanted to see the body or say goodbye afterwards. Some had spoken up and said they wanted to do these things, but someone had persuaded them it wasn't a good idea.

It had never even occurred to me that I'd want to see the body. That seems a bit gruesome to me. Other folk spoke of looking after the person who had died, laid out in their own home, and how helpful they had found it. They said it gave them time to get used to the person being dead and gave them a chance to say goodbye properly. What they said had a big impact on me and got me wondering what would be best for you folks and for Joy too. Maybe I'm being thoughtless, making a decision like that on my own.

One of the reasons I thought of a quick 'disposal' was that with some of you so far away, I had the thought that rather than you all flying here on expensive last-minute tickets for a funeral, my body could be cremated and then you could come over for a decent holiday a while later and have a celebration then—whether you'll be celebrating the life I had or the fact I've gone only you'll know!

The thing that kept coming up was the importance of taking time. Somebody actually suggested that you don't necessarily need the body for this ... it's just that it provides a focus for everyone. The other thing was listening, really listening to what you each really need, and making sure that the quiet, shy and stunned-into-silence ones are heard too. There was a suggestion that a friend might be helpful for that—someone not quite so involved. I'm open to all your thoughts and ideas on this.

With modern technology, maybe you could sit with the person who died through a video stream. You could dip in and out, see and hear what's going on—even rewind it if you missed a good joke or story—and not need to fly halfway round the world until you really want to.

Have a think about this. I would really appreciate knowing your points of view. I have had an amazing life so far and plan on a good bit more, as you know, so when I do go, I'll be ready. I would be happy if you were able to celebrate all that we had together and then get on with your amazing lives, knowing I am happy wherever I am.

Big hugs to you all,
Pa

Getting Help To Record Your Wishes

It can be beneficial asking someone not so close to help record your wishes and also to help facilitate a conversation with those who will be carrying out your wishes. Lin recounts how she did this with Susie and her daughter:

"Susie's daughter was visiting from England when Susie suddenly became unwell. After a night in hospital she recovered, but her daughter felt unsettled by what had happened. I have known Susie for many years and happened to meet her daughter the next day. After a conversation about death and dying, I offered to meet with both of them so that they could talk about Susie's wishes.

"We began by outlining our spiritual beliefs, which gave context to the details being discussed, and then I took notes so that Susie and her daughter could concentrate on the conversation. We agreed that, when practical, it will be good to meet with Susie's son to go through what Susie wants at her funeral and to read the poems together. Susie's son is a saxophonist, and they had already planned for him to play a piece of music at Susie's burial. Her daughter is a silk painter and wants to make a personalised silk cover for Susie's coffin. She intends to make it soon and give it to her mum so that Susie can enjoy it for a while. Afterwards, it will become a family memento.

"The conversation took about an hour and a half. I typed up the notes and circulated them, so now Susie, her daughter, her son, her carer and a friend all have copies, and her wishes are widely known."

Here are the notes from Lin's meeting with Susie and her daughter:

Susie wants a cardboard coffin so that people can write things on it and decorate it—a cardboard coffin as plain, simple and inexpensive as possible. A local funeral director is known to have supplied one in the past. Susie wants to wear her very well-worn, much-darned, biodegradable, rainbow alpaca jumper—she wants to be cosy.

Susie feels that there is something special about leaving from home for the last time. She would like her body to lie at home in her studio. Her daughter feels that she is okay with this, with the support that her mum has arranged. The silk cover can be laid over the coffin, without a lid, so that anyone who wants to can draw it back to see Susie's face. Susie's art pieces are to be gifted to any family or friend who wants them.

Susie's bear, Ming, wants to be buried with Susie, wearing his woollen hat and socks. Her bronze Highland pony, Windy, is to be her headstone at her grave. Susie wants to be buried at the local natural burial ground, with a small gathering of close friends and family present. She keeps an envelope in her desk drawer with details of the music, songs and poems she would like.

Susie would like her dates, 1935–?, added to the public bench, which she funded some years ago and which she sees as a place of family legacy.

Susie has the handwoven, vegetable-dyed, silk sash of the family's clan. Her wish is that this becomes a family heirloom.

Expressing Your Wishes in a Letter

As we said earlier in the chapter, we believe letters can be helpfully used to encourage and support those who will be involved in the days after our last breath. Your wishes could also be expressed by recording a video or audio message. We recommend giving guidance rather than specifics.

Before you begin, if you have specific requests, roughly cost out what you are asking for and think about who will pay for it at the time. Bear in mind that bank accounts are frozen upon a person's death, so unless you have a joint account, no one will be able to use money in your account at the time. Banks are used to paying funeral directors' invoices directly, but it may be more difficult if you are considering alternatives. If you have appointed someone to make arrangements for after your last breath—see Chapter 11—you could consider setting up a joint account with them specifically for this purpose.

Also think about whom your letter is for and when you expect them to read it, and make sure people know about the letter and its contents. If they do not know about it and find it too late, it could be distressing for those to whom it was addressed.

When you come to write your letter, it could have these elements in it:

1. **A reference to your beliefs** regarding what happens after your last breath. It can be surprising how little others know of our beliefs.

2. **Explanations to those significant to you about how they might react.** Death is such an unfamiliar experience for many people nowadays that most do not know how they will react to someone's death. Your explanation of how they might react might be invaluable when the time comes.

3. **Encouragement and suggestions to the people who will be significantly affected by your death for taking care of themselves** in the first few days. Again, most of us are unfamiliar with death, and traditional funeral practises focus on the funeral rather than on feelings or taking time with the person who has taken their last breath. This means people may be ill-prepared to look after themselves in the first few days.

4. **Guidance on your preferred options** for the care of your body after your last breath and whether you want burial or cremation. Would you prefer a funeral or a community ceremony or service, and would you like a celebrant or a funeral director to be involved? Knowing your preferred options ahead of time allows people to get used to ideas that may well be new to them and to explore how they might carry them out with you or for you. If you have opted out of organ or tissue donation, you might include this information. It is also very helpful to include what you have no particular preferences about.

5. **Encouragement to arrange meaningful get-togethers** for both family and friends in the first few days after your last breath and before your burial or cremation. It is common, for various reasons, that friends do not have so much contact in the period immediately before someone dies and so it is particularly worth considering how to incorporate a meaningful get-together to give friends the opportunity to say goodbye.

As you can see, all these elements are for guidance. It is our experience that, given time and encouragement, people know what best serves them in the days after someone's last breath. By giving guidance, you provide them with the scope to do what is best for them whilst also honouring your requests and preferences. We encourage you to revisit and perhaps revise your letter every time there is a significant change in your circumstances or every five years, whichever is sooner.

Here are two different responses to the ideas in this chapter. The first is an example kindly shared by Freya:

I write this letter to help guide those who have care of my body after I have died. I hope you have known me in life and so can read this letter holding the knowledge you have of me. But maybe you don't know me, and if so, I ask you simply to do what you can according to the circumstances you find yourselves in. My wishes would be that someone sits with my body for a while after I finish breathing and gives me their honest company as I let go of being me. If you can do this, then thank you for that intimate kindness. You don't have to do anything except just pause, sit and be yourself. I hope, in a small way, this will also help you adjust to the experience of finding me dead.

Following that, I would want little fuss, so dispose of my body as cheaply as possible, and if you can be homemade or green in the process, then that would be wonderful. Avoid social formalities, religion, headstones and hearses.

If I have family or friends still living, please call them and pass them this letter.

To my loved ones:

Firstly, I thank you all for the love you have given me. Know the love that I have for you. Our loving has given my life meaning and value. Forgive me for times I have hurt you or let you down, and I forgive you if there is anything you hold uneasiness with. If you want to remember me, notice the things you know I have held as precious: the beauty in the world; the simplicity and complexity of natural form; the light falling; the colours shifting; the tide turning; the seasons changing; the warmth of a smile; the remarkable creative industry our hearts and minds allow us; a handful of nuts; a taste of whiskey; and an autumn russet. When alive, at my most peaceful, I believed that I was the same momentary flicker of presence that is within all things. In remembering what we experienced together, my flicker remains with you—perhaps my love can even return to you when you are feeling alone or in need. And remember to call my name if you need to play a good hand of canasta.

Spend time with my body, if you can, for a while after I die. I would like this company, and I hope you can slowly begin to say goodbye to my life during that time. Look after yourself; attend to what you need. Share this watching with others if you can, and share your memories with humour and sadness. If this can be at my home, then well and good, but whatever is possible is fine.

After that, dispose of my body as you see fit. Be mindful of my belief that less is often more. You can gather friends together, or have a ritual walk or picnic if you want to, any time after I die. Do something outside if you can.

If no one has a strong preference with what to do with my body, and there is money in my account to cover this, I would like to be wrapped in a clean sheet and buried in a plain cardboard coffin. Draw or write on the cardboard if you want. Use a local natural burial ground. I would choose an oak tree if planting a tree is allowed there. If you want a name marker, the sites sell you one, but I don't care. If you opt to cremate me, put the ashes somehow back into the earth. Maybe I have crafted a small memory box that you could also bury somewhere that is meaningful to you.

I will walk with you.

Freya

And now an example kindly shared by John:

To whom it may concern,

If you are reading this, then I've either moved onto what I will call here my 'Soul Home'—it's not my name for it, but it will suffice as a generic term, and you may well have your own name for the place where you may believe our souls go to after death, and you may have your own view of what that might be like just as I have mine, but that's not necessarily relevant today—or if I haven't yet journeyed, then I am likely to be almost there but perhaps not able to communicate with you in this place. In simple terms, to this world, I have died or am actively in the process of dying, so I am writing to help you with planning for this and for the disposal of my body.

I can't know who is reading this letter. You may have a lot of knowledge about me, or some, or even very little or none. My knowledge of you is likely to be fairly similar to yours of me, so I will write as if we know little of each other. If you do know me, then nothing will come as a surprise, but my wishes, as expressed here, may not fully tie in with your needs at this time. That's OK because it's appropriate to prioritise your needs over mine. This is a guide to what I would want; it's not an instruction manual.

One quite important thing to know about me is my spirituality. It might not be yours—you may not even feel you have one, and that's OK by me, but I do. I'm an animist, so I believe everything has spirit and in many cases is a spirit. Feel free to explore the concept, or not, as you will, but be aware that this core spirituality underlies this letter and my wishes.

If at any time you are uncertain or feel you may need support or guidance, then feel free to seek it. There are undertakers, morticians, burial grounds, soul midwives, death doulas and companions as well as animists out there who can assist. Even Google and Wiki can help, assuming these aren't archaic terms to you.

I'm going to cover four main areas: The Period of Dying or Unpacking for the Journey; Caring For the Body and Soul during the Journey or The Journey Time; Funerary Time; and Caring For Yourselves Afterwards.

Unpacking for the Journey:
I'm hoping my departure point will be my own home—the place loved by Bridget and me, and the place where I will have built relationships with the building, the land and those and that which live there. The spirit and spirits of place. If that hasn't been

possible, then please try to bring some things from there to where I am dying—maybe one of my Penjing trees or groves. Bring the feel of the place to me.

Bridget often joked that I'd want the Hu playing their blend of Mongolian folk metal at the end or perhaps the pounding drums of Saor Patrol, but actually I would want to listen to Carolyn Hillyer, and at the very end, quietly play her journey song 'Fare You Well (Heron Fly You Home)'. If you are there as I finally leave my body, be there with the music. Let it play a few times more and share the space with my spirit. If you don't have such a belief, then share the space with the music, and take a chance to just breathe before needing to.

The Journey Time:

Again, I'd like for my body to lie at the place I call home so that those who would wish to bid me farewell on my journey can do so. That would include the spirits of the place who will know me. It would be nice to have any of my Penjing trees with me that are not yet planted into the earth. I would ask that they then be planted appropriately in the place I have called home—they will hold the memory of their relationships with me in that place. If possible, before my body is taken, I would like to lie outside there, open to the elements, for the place to know of my passing even if only briefly.

Funerary Time:

If my beloved Bridget has died before me, then you will have her ashes. I would wish them to be placed in a biodegradable urn and for this to be held in my hands on my chest in the place of my interment. If I own a piece of woodland, then this is where I would wish to be buried—if not, then in a natural burial ground. If Bridget is still alive, then please ensure, should she so wish, that her ashes are placed into my burial place when it is her time.

I would wish the service to be animistic in nature and for my casket to be bio-degradable and painted with natural pigments, reflecting scenes of the land—of these blessed islands—painted by anyone who wants to paint. There is no requirement for artistic expertise, only the desire to give to my journey. Such will be my 'grave goods'.

Caring For Yourselves Afterwards:

Take all the time and space you need. There are likely to be tears, but let there also be wonder, joy and laughter amongst those tears. There will be strong emotions about, so please remember that accord is so much more pleasurable than discord.

Feel my breath in the wind, my touch in the water, my support in the earth, my warmth in the sun during the day and my joy in the moon at night.

Blessings,

John

21

Responding Creatively

When someone significant in your life dies, it is not always possible to be present. There are all sorts of reasons why this may happen. Even though someone very much wants to be there, it may not be physically possible due to distance, finances, work or other commitments. It may be that someone is close by, but they are prevented from being there because relationships are difficult. Also, when a death is unexpected even when someone is physically close by and wants to be there, the investigation process can mean not having access to the person's body.

Sometimes, your own circumstances may prevent you from being present in person, and you may create your own way of being present from a distance. You do not have to be there in person to be part of what is happening; you only need to be engaged in it. If you know that others are gathering at a particular time, you could join them from wherever you are by finding a quiet place, giving your attention to the gathering and following your instincts in doing what is right for you.

In this chapter, we share stories of how people have taken care of themselves in these situations. Please be aware that some of these stories are of situations in which people were distressed.

Including Close Friends
When someone is ill at the end of their life, friends may have

less contact with them. On the other hand, friends may be involved in caring for a person in the last weeks or months. Sometimes, as happened with Diana, the friends step back when family arrive in the person's final days. So how can friends say goodbye if they have not had the opportunity to do this before someone dies?

Jenny's story is one example of what is possible. Her close friends had not been able to visit her during her last weeks. She was going to be buried in a family burial ground many miles away from her home, with a local memorial service later for her large circle of friends. After her last breath and before her final journey across Scotland, Jenny was brought to a yurt in the woods. This gave her close friends time to say goodbye.

Jenny was a nature lover, so this place was particularly appropriate for her. Her sister brought some treasured possessions, and her friends made a memory table with these and cards that other friends had sent to her. While the space was being prepared, the idea came to invite friends to give Jenny an offering from the woodland. So the invitation was placed by her coffin with a pair of secateurs.

Some people who came to visit Jenny stayed with her for just five minutes, while others stayed for a long time. People said afterwards that this was a poignant and beautiful activity for them, walking in the woods, thinking about Jenny and then putting their offering with her in her coffin.

When a Death is Unexpected

The suddenness of an unexpected death compounds what can be a complicated and stressful time. We have heard of people having difficulties due to official procedures preventing contact when a death is unexpected. Should you find yourself in such a situation, we encourage you to find someone who can support you in your dealings with the police and other officials. We encourage you to do what you can to look after yourself and let others look after you. Small, intentional gatherings can benefit everyone affected by the person's unexpected death.

Isabel generously shared with us what happened when her son Ben died suddenly and unexpectedly in his home when he was 30 years old. Although Ben had lived with a life-long life-limiting illness, he grew up living life to the full, developed a good career and played music with a band in his spare time.

One Sunday lunchtime, Isabel received a phone call from Ben, who was in distress. She called 999 and then drove 30 minutes to Ben's flat, where she was met with fire officers trying to get access at the rear of the building and through the front door because no one had a key. The doctor attending took her next door to a restaurant to wait until they heard the sound of the front door being broken open. Then, Isabel had to wait in Ben's living room until, after a time, the doctor came to say that they had done everything they could, but Ben had died. Isabel so much wanted to see Ben, but the doctor said she could not because they had to wait for the police to arrive.

Later, a detective explained that, as it was a sudden and unexpected death, there would be an investigation and that Isabel was not able to see him as she might contaminate the evidence. She was taken to a local police station, where she was asked questions about Ben that she felt were intrusive and insensitive. It was late that evening when she got home.

A few days later, Isabel had to go to the mortuary to identify Ben, who was propped on his side on a trolley behind a glass window. The post-mortem examination later confirmed that Ben had died due to his illness.

Fortunately, Isabel felt well supported by the funeral

director who had been recommended to her. However, when she visited Ben, she was disturbed to find herself unable to put her arms around him because she could not reach him in his coffin. She said she only went once because she could not bear to visit and then have to leave him again.

At the time, Isabel got comfort from Ben's best friend and members of Ben's family carrying out her son's wishes: they created a football-themed funeral, with Ben's guitar lying on his coffin.

However, Isabel says there are things she would have done differently if she had known then what she knows now. Firstly, she would have asked for Ben to be laid on a lower table at the funeral director's premises so that she could reach in to hug him. Secondly, rather than have the funeral at the crematorium, she would have held it at a hall and invited the rest of the band to play.

When Relationships are Difficult

It is not always the case that you want to connect with the person who has died, either shortly after their last breath or at a funeral. Maybe it feels like you can't be there, you can't face being there or you don't want to be there. This could be because of your relationship with the person who has died or someone else connected with them. The situation may feel uncomfortable or complicated. Maybe you can't be there because you need to protect yourself. If your instinct is to not be there, trust that and honour it. People who have been in such situations have told us they did not want to be involved.

We aim to inform and inspire you and perhaps even give you the courage to do what is right for you. We are very grateful to bring you Deirdre's story of how she approached the death of her father, who had sexually abused her and her brothers and sisters as children. The damage caused by the abuse then affected her choices when her aunt, who she was very close to, also died.

"Lots of my friends don't know about the abuse … it's not the sort of thing that comes up in conversation. I was working with people who had been sexually abused when the memories came back. When it is abuse by a parent, there is a particular level of betrayal, which makes it hard to trust anybody. I was lucky and was able to tap into good healing so that I could function in the world, and I learned that holding on to it was only going to damage me more.

"I came to a place of deep acceptance, so when my father had a major heart attack, I went to see him in hospital, knowing he might die any time. I said, 'I know everything that happened with all the family. I know what you have done. I have come to say goodbye.' I was very courageous. I knew I wouldn't see him again. So I said goodbye and gave myself permission for that to be the last time I visited.

"When there is abuse like this, you grieve the loss of him, the father he should have been, and you grieve the loss of what you thought the world was made of a long time before he dies. So when he died a few years later, I chose not to attend his funeral. There was no relationship there. However, I was very close to my aunt, his sister, and when she died, I was very torn about what to do. I wanted to go to her funeral, but it meant coming into contact with other members of the family, which stirred difficult feelings in me. So in the end, I decided not to go.

"I thought of my aunt and asked myself, 'What would she want me to do about the funeral?', and the answer was to not put myself through it. I knew what time her funeral was, so I created a space with candles and special things for myself and linked in with her from home. I had a sense of clear, direct communication between us, and I feel very satisfied with what I did.

"If my story has affected you and you would like to talk

with someone, I suggest you contact The Survivors Trust, which is a nationwide survivors' network, for help."

Resolving Regrets

We are aware that reading this book might have brought up regrets for you as you think of things you could have done differently. Also, when you share this information with others, you could bring up regrets for them too. This was Lin's experience when she and Kate were writing the 'After the Last Breath' course for Pushing Up the Daisies:

"After a week with all of us there with her, I thought I was fine about all that had happened when my mum died in hospital following a fall. Nearly two years later, I woke before it got light, feeling restless. So I went a long walk and found sobs and tears and then feelings of such disappointment that I had not done more to bring her home before she died. I was frustrated that I had not even raised the subject of bringing her home after she died. By bringing her home, the house could have said goodbye, and we could have said goodbye, with her friends and neighbours and our wider family, over tea and cake, taking the time we needed. However, it was the right decision, at the time, for her to stay in the hospital. We had no idea how to get Mum home, never mind how to negotiate doing so with the hospital staff. At the time, it was the right thing to do.

"Writing the course with Kate, two years after this experience, showed me possibilities which were new to me, so my regret resurfaced. I asked a friend, who is good at listening, to help me re-imagine the whole thing, dreaming up help to get Mum home from hospital and to care for her in her house. In my mind, I saw myself tending to Mum's body after her last breath, with others who wanted to do this. I imagined spending time with family, friends and neighbours around Mum, talking about her and making music around her. In my imagination, we were able to complete things by filling in Mum's grave ourselves.

"This process involved three sessions of about an hour each, about a week apart. My friend mostly just listened as I told her this new version of what had happened. If you have a friend who is good at listening, perhaps you could do something similar, or you might find a professional listener to help you, like a therapist or counsellor. You might write the experience you would like to have had as a story or draw sketches of the moments that feel important to you. Trust your instincts to create whatever you need to address your regrets.

"I feel that when I know someone, in a subtle way, I breathe with them. When they take their last breath, I pause my breathing a little, too, until I can learn what the rhythm of my own breathing is without them. It is as though I held my breath a bit when Mum took her last one, and I did not start to breathe fully again.

"It is never too late to give yourself the experience you need. This was a conscious process over three weeks. I took my time, noticed how I felt and found that the next stage of the story came to me. What had been a non-experience, an empty few days, has been replaced with rich and often joyful memories. I feel I have completed and made right, for myself, my farewell to my mum. And I can breathe fully again."

Spontaneous Responses

We have learned that conscious activity can be helpful, in a considered or a spontaneous way. Kate recalls her experience with a friend who wasn't invited to the funeral of her ex-partner's mother:

"A few years ago, when a good friend was visiting me, her ex-partner's mother died. She was very upset about her death, having had a close relationship with her for a long time. Since she wasn't invited to the funeral, we decided to make a ritual ourselves to help my friend. It was completely homemade and spontaneous, using what we had available. We decided our intention would be for my friend to say goodbye. That afternoon, she spent time writing a letter to her ex-partner's mother. I spent the time decorating a room with flowers, candles and fairy lights, creating a nice atmosphere. Then, in the evening, we went into the room, my friend lit the candles and we put on music they had listened to together. I said, 'We are gathered to say goodbye to …', and my friend read her letter and let the tears flow. We sang some songs they had sung together, and then she blew out the candles.

"The next day, my friend said how much lighter and more whole she felt. She had released the anger and hurt that not attending the funeral had caused. Neither of us had ever thought about or studied making rituals. It is interesting to think how we instinctively did what she needed to do."

It can be some time after a person dies that we realise we want to say good-bye. Know that it is never too late to pay conscious attention to what happens after the last breath of someone significant in your life. Sometimes life is full-on, and you simply keep going and accept that you cannot be there to say goodbye. This is what happened to Lin:

"Some years ago, when I was living in Gloucestershire, an article I read inspired me to spend a day tree planting in the Scottish Borders. It was in September, and my grandma came to mind as I drove north. Her birthday had been in September, and she had also died in that month, some twelve years previously. Being very pregnant at the time, I had not travelled north for her funeral.

"I was given a bag of saplings to plant. They were rowan trees, which are also known as mountain ash trees.

As I took one out of the bag, I had a strong memory of watching my chain-smoker grandma sitting at the table, a cigarette, as always, between her lips, with the ash growing steadily longer until one of us said, 'Your ash is going to fall, Grandma!', and she would catch it in her hand as it did. I looked at the little tree, laughed at the thought of her 'mountin' ash' and said, 'This one's for you, Grandma!'

"So there is a mountain ash tree somewhere in the Carrifran valley that commemorates her. I had had no intention of commemorating her until that moment and did not know I needed or wanted to. It just happened, and it gave me great joy."

22

Pause and Ponder

One of the best ways to take care of ourselves is to think in advance about what is important to us and how we may achieve what we need when someone close to us dies. When we began writing this book, we had no idea how it would grow and develop from its early beginnings. We had spoken many times of wanting people to know what was possible when someone dies so they could make informed decisions that supported their well-being. Three years later, we have learned so much from finding the answers to the questions that people asked us and from those that we asked ourselves.

Questions have been key to this process, so in this final chapter, we offer the opportunity to explore some for yourself. In this book, we have encouraged you to slow down when someone dies. Now, we want to bring that approach to the closing of this book, giving space to each question. We invite you to take time to ponder all that you have read and if, and how, it has changed the way you might approach things when someone important to you dies.

Does considering death as a process rather than an event affect how you may respond to it?

How does knowing the details of what physically happens to someone's body after their last breath affect you?

Could that make a difference to the choices you make when someone dies?

Have you ever considered spending time with someone after their last breath at home? Does it feel important to you?

What would be your priorities in the days before and during the burial or cremation of someone significant to you?

Would taking charge, when someone dies, have benefits for you? Are there any aspects you don't feel able to take charge of?

Tending to someone's body is not for everyone. Is it for you? Do you know a trusted source of advice that could help you?

Would you consider bringing someone home from hospital after their last breath? Who in your circle of family and friends might support you in doing this?

Would you be comfortable transporting someone on a board, wrapped in a blanket, or would you want them to be in a coffin? What are the practical considerations in your house for access and moving around a coffin?

We wanted to include a question to ponder about unexpected death but could not find a helpful one. Then, we remembered that people learn first aid so that they can use it, if necessary, while hoping they will never need to. In that spirit, we encourage you to consider the unthinkable and reread Chapter 12. Take in, as best you can, the information and guidance in it. That way, if you or someone around you is ever in that situation, you will be as prepared as possible to look after yourself and to look out for anyone else involved.

What does the symbolism of crossing the threshold mean to you?

Think about when someone significant to you took their last breath.

How did you react in the first moments and hours?

How did others around you react?

What personal dynamics were there?

What relationships were affected?

How could you look after yourself when someone dies? What support might you need at that time? How could you prepare yourself, or others around you, in advance?

Might you have difficulty making your voice heard when someone important to you dies? Does involving people you know feel helpful to you or intrusive? Would you be likely to get busy and distracted from emotions?

Who might you need to look out for? Do you think that you, or anyone in your close circle, would benefit from taking time to hand someone over when they die?

Take time to think about situations where you have not been able to be there after someone special to you took their last breath. Choosing one, devise a conscious activity to say something you did not have a chance to say and carry it out. How does it feel to create and do it?

In what ways might you start conversations with your friends and family about your wishes when you die? What might you include in a letter to express your wishes for the days immediately after your last breath? Are you ready to write it?

Whether you have dipped into this book to find something out or have read it cover to cover, we hope it has given you an understanding of the benefits of slowing down when someone dies. We want you to know that you can still hug someone and speak to them in the days after their last breath, and that it can be really comforting to do so. We want you to have the opportunity to hand someone over in your own time, when you know in your bones that something has changed forever, and everything is okay. We believe that many people are ready to take charge of what happens when someone dies and that, in time, this will become the norm.

May your next experience of death be a meaningful one.

Kate and Lin, 2023

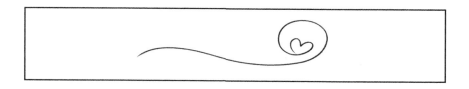

Appendix 1:
End-of-Life Companions

End-of-life companions and local organisations providing compassionate care to people who are dying are becoming increasingly available in Scotland. They can support people living alone and also those with people around them. They can be helpful if you face death without someone to tend to your body and soul in the way that you wish for after your last breath.

Soul Midwives and Death Doulas
Soul midwives and death doulas are non-medical companions for people who are dying. They work alongside someone at the end of life to try to achieve the kind of death they would like, if possible. Their work is very similar, with the different names reflecting different training pathways.

We spoke to Jude Meryl about her work as a soul midwife. She said, "I feel it is an immense privilege to be there at the end of someone's life. In the last two years, I have noticed a marked rise in interest in our work, with a steady stream of people wanting both to know more and to support the work.

"Individual soul midwives will choose the scope of their work. They might work with individuals at home or in a hospice, hospital or care home; they might be retained by a hospice to work with their patients or be involved in a hospital bedside-companion scheme. There are soul midwives who are also birth midwives and some who work with babies and children when they die.

"Often, they will first meet with a person who has had a terminal diagnosis, and then there may be an interval when they do not meet until the person becomes frailer and in need of support. How much the soul midwife may become involved will depend on whether the person is alone or has friends and family supporting them.

"Soul midwives support those of any faith, working with whatever beliefs the person has or does not have. Being able to discuss the person's beliefs can be really helpful. As the time of death approaches, it can be valuable to reflect back to the person what they said about their beliefs.

"We recognise that death is a process and have a non-medical framework to describe the stages. We have processes to ease the transition from one stage to the next, such as exploring the person's final wishes at the end of life, doing memory work, like creating photo albums and recipe books, or anticipating important events they might not be present at and preparing cards or gifts.

"As the person becomes increasingly frail, the soul midwife's role is one of deep listening, with the heart, to what is said and what is not said. At this stage, old trauma can surface to be healed, and creative visualisation might be used to provide tools to ease anxiety. In our training, we are made aware of the importance of dreams and visions of loved ones who are already dead, which the person who is dying may experience. Such visions are recognised as an indication that death may not be far away and, if validated, are overwhelmingly a source of reassurance and comfort to the person in their last days.

"Once the person is spending more time sleeping than waking, the soul midwife will make the surroundings as familiar and supportive as possible and might use soothing touch on the hands and feet. In the final days, when breathing might be difficult, we help to calm the person with breathing techniques. After the last breath, if the person has requested it, we might sit vigil with the person, alone or with the family."

Community Organisations

A slowly increasing number of community organisations provide voluntary companionship to people at the end of their life. No One Dies Alone (NODA) Ayrshire is one such example. NODA offers emotional support to help relieve the loneliness and isolation of anyone in Ayrshire dealing with end-of-life issues. They also provide training for individuals and organisations to help with the spiritual care of the dying. Their trained and experienced volunteers are compassionate and work intuitively to hold a loving space for those who need it. This includes both the person who is dying and their families who may need the comfort of a companion to be with them. They offer vigiling, one-to-one support, group support, bereavement counselling and end-of-life training and body care at home after death. Their ethos is to make a difference locally by training, empowering and supporting ordinary members of the community to help each other at the end of life, working at many different levels to instigate this change and to bring back a sense of care and naturalness to death, dying and bereavement. They accept referrals from anyone and can be contacted through their website at www.nodaa.org.uk.

Appendix 2: Supportive Essential Oils and Flower Essences

Essential Oils

Essential oils are made from physical plant material and are for external use only when diluted with a suitable carrier oil or lotion. We find essential oils helpful in slowing the natural transformation processes, as an insect repellent and to create a clear, calm and supportive atmosphere.

Those we most commonly use are as follows:

Lavender, for its antibacterial properties and also for its calming effect on the people around. It can be added to water for washing and dripped around the person's body.

Frankincense, which is a sacred oil, beautifully suited to the situation for its calming properties and to support soul transition. It is used in our oil blends and in room diffusers.

Cedarwood is an insect repellent, used in our body-oil blend and dripped around the body and on a cloth covering the face.

Body Oil Blend

Mix together 30ml of olive oil or another carrier oil with:
    4 drops of frankincense essential oil
    4 drops of cedarwood essential oil
    6 drops of neroli light essential oil

Gently apply to the person's skin after their last breath.

Supportive Blend
We use this blend to provide comfort and support through times of grief and change. It can be prepared in two convenient ways.

For aroma salts, half fill a 10ml bottle with Himalayan salt and add:
5 drops of frankincense oil
5 drops of rosewood oil
8 drops of mandarin oil
Give it a good shake, and keep it in your pocket to breathe in at moments when you need to clear and support your mind.

For a roller ball or bottle, mix together 10ml of jojoba or another carrier oil with:
1 drop of frankincense essential oil
1 drop of rosewood essential oil
2 drops of mandarin essential oil
Apply it to your skin when you need to clear and support your mind.

Flower Essences
As flower essences work on the emotional level, they are beautifully suited to help support the wide range of emotions that may be encountered at this time. They are gentle, but powerful, vibrational catalysts that transform negative emotions into positive ones. Flower essences are made from the non-physical aspect of the plant and are, despite the name, not related to essential oils.

They are safe to be taken internally, either directly from the bottle or added to drinks. They can also be added to a spray bottle to spray yourself, the person who has died and the room. You can add essences to the washing water for someone's body as an extra act of love. You can also incorporate them into any balms to anoint their body. The most well-known blend of essences is Bach's Rescue Remedy. This excellent first-aid remedy for shock or acute distress can be obtained from most high street pharmacies and is always in our bag.

Other Bach essences that could be helpful, depending on your emotional state, are as follows:

Cerato, for lack of confidence to follow one's own judgement. Cerato brings faith and confidence to trust our own inner guidance and be quietly self-reliant.

Elm, for overwhelm. Elm brings back positive qualities of unshakeable reliability and inner resilience and restores the ability to cope.

Impatiens, for impatience and irritability, especially with others. Impatiens brings patience, calm, tolerance and understanding of others.

Pine, for guilt and blaming oneself for feeling things have gone wrong. Pine brings inner forgiveness and restores self-worth.

Death's Door Essences. Healing Grief helps you to stay clear, aligned and grounded while processing grief. It is available from www.deaths-door.co.uk.

Other ranges of flower essences are available, such as Alaskan Essences and Bailey Essences.

References

Abarbanel, A. (2017) *Grief and Adjustment To Change: A No-Nonsense Approach Volume 1 of Fully Human Psychopathy Tools for Life Series.* Amazon Digital Services LLC – KDP Print US.

Abraham-Hicks (2023) *Abraham-Hicks Publications* [Online]. Available at: https://www.abraham-hicks.com/(Accessed: 07-March-2023).

Anderson, M. (2005) *Attending the Dying: A Handbook of Practical Guidelines.* Barcelona: Morehouse Publishing.

Brean, J. (2018) *Millennials are more likely to believe in an afterlife than are older generations: Do you believe in life after—well—life?* [Online]. Available at: https://nationalpost.com/news/canada/millennials-do-you-believe-in-life-after-life (Accessed: 24-March-2023).

Callender, R. et al. (eds) (2012) *The Natural Death Handbook.* Fifth edition. London, Strange Attractor.

Chapple, A. and Ziebland, S. (2010) 'Viewing the body after bereavement due to a traumatic death: qualitative study in the UK', *The British Medical Journal,* 340:c2032.

Child Bereavement UK (2023) *Support and guidance* [Online]. Available at https://www.childbereavementuk.org/ (Accessed: 07-March-2023).

Fenwick, P. and Fenwick, E. (2008) *The Art of Dying.* London, Continuum.

Mannix, K. (2021) *Listen: How to Find the Words for Tender Conversations.* Glasgow, William Collins.

Mowll, J., Lobb, E.A. and Wearing, M. (2017) 'The transformative meanings of viewing or not viewing the body after sudden death', *Death Studies,* 40(1), pp. 45-53 [Online]. Available at: https://www.tandfonline.com/doi/full/10.1080/07481187.2015.1059385 (Accessed: 31-March-2023).

Naturally Useful (2023) *New hands weaving old ways* [Online]. Available at https://www.naturallyuseful.co.uk/ (Accessed: 31-March-2023).

No One Dies Alone Ayrshire (2023) *Noda Services* [Online]. Available at: https://www.nodaa.org.uk/our-services (Accessed: 07-March-2023).

Poer, N.J. (2002) *Living Into Dying: A Journal of Spiritual and Practical Death Care for Family and Community.* Ontario, White Feather Publishing.

Pozhitkov, A.E. et al. (2017) 'Tracing the dynamics of gene transcripts after organismal death', *Open Biology,* 7(1) [Online]. Available at: https://royalsocietypublishing.org/doi/10.1098/rsob.160267 (Accessed: 08-March-2023).

Public Health England (2018) *Statistical Commentary: End of Life Care Profiles, February 2018 Update.* [Online]. Available at: https://www.gov.uk/government/statistics/end-of-life-care-profiles-february-2018-update/statistical-commentary-end-of-life-care-profiles-february-2018-update (Accessed: 28-March-2023).

Pushing Up the Daisies (2023) *Information* [Online]. Available at: https://pushingupthedaisies.org.uk/information/ (Accessed: 27-March-2023).

Roper Center (2014) *Paradise Polled: Americans and the Afterlife* [Online]. Available at: https://ropercenter.cornell.edu/paradise-polled-americans-and-afterlife (Accessed 24-March-2023).

Scottish Government (2020) *Scottish household survey 2019: annual report* [Online]. Available at https://www.gov.scot/publications/scottish-household-survey-2019-annual-report/ (Accessed: 24-March-2023).

Scottish Government (2022) *Tell Us Once* [Online]. Available at: https://www.mygov.scot/tell-us-once (Accessed: 27-March-2023).

Scottish Government (2023) *Births, deaths and family* [Online]. Available at: https://www.mygov.scot/browse/births-deaths-marriages (Accessed 10-March-2023).

Scottish Government (2023) *Cremation: statutory forms* [Online]. Available at: https://www.gov.scot/publications/cremation-statutory-forms/ (Accessed: 07-March-2023).

Talmud Yerushalmi. Moed Katan 3:5.

The Centre for Sacred Deathcare (2023) *Ritual skills training for death doulas and others* [Online]. Available at: https://sacreddeathcare.com/ (Accessed: 07-Match-2023).

The Crown Office and Procurator Fiscal Service (2023) *Support and services* [Online]. Available at: https://www.copfs.gov.uk/services/ bereavement-support/guide-for-bereaved-family-members/ (Accessed: 07-March-2023).

The Good Funeral Guide (2021) *Where do you begin?* [Online]. Available at: https://www.goodfuneralguide.co.uk/ (Accessed: 24-March-2023).

Theos (2008) *Four in Ten People Believe in Ghosts* [Online]. Available at: https://www.theosthinktank.co.uk/comment/2009/04/13/four-in-ten-people-believe-in-ghosts (24-March-2023).

The Survivors Trust (2000) *Contact Us* [Online]. Available at: https://www.thesurvivorstrust.org/contact (Accessed: 27-March-2023)

Winston's Wish (2023) *Get bereavement support* [Online]. Available at: https://www.winstonswish.org/supporting-you/ (Accessed: 07-March-2023).

Body Care Manual

In this manual, we explain all the practical steps you might want to take when tending to the body of someone who has taken their last breath. Reading through this could feel daunting, but please remember that these are our suggestions for how to do things if you want to take these steps.

If there is no smell from body fluids around the person's body and you know they will not be in the home for more than a couple of days, then there is no need to do anything other than reduce bedding to a light cover and keep the room cool.

If you intend to have the person's body in the home for more than a couple of days, and especially if there are any caution signs, it is a priority to reduce the bedclothes and cool the person's tummy with cool packs as soon as possible after their last breath.

If you are at all nervous, contact someone who can support you over the phone or in person. It is perfectly respectful to cover someone's body and leave the room to seek advice at any time. Practical body care is not for everyone, and if you do not want to do it, you do not need to read this manual. There will be nurses, carers and other experienced people in your community who can assist, so there is no need to push yourself to do something you would prefer not to do.

It is not essential to close the eyes or mouth or replace dentures. However, most people will instinctively want to do this. If this is to be done, it is usually best to do it in the first few hours after the person's last breath and before their body becomes stiff with rigor mortis. Wait until a health professional has verified the death before doing anything other than closing the eyes and mouth, replacing dentures and checking that the continence pad is clean and dry.

Understanding Rigor Mortis

Rigor mortis is muscle stiffening due to changes in muscle cell metabolism when the cells do not receive oxygen. It usually begins 4–6 hours after someone's last breath. It eases after a day or two, after which the body becomes permanently floppy.

You can first notice rigor mortis starting in the smaller muscles of the face. Depending on how long it is since the person took their last breath, rigor mortis may be present, which makes it more difficult to manoeuvre their limbs. However, by gently massaging their muscles and joints, you can ease their stiffness so that you can move them more easily. You might feel like you could cause damage, but this is very unlikely.

Before Your Begin:
If you wish to proceed with tending to someone's body, please first read Chapter 15: Before You Begin Tending To a Body.

> Make sure the atmosphere in the room is as comfortable and supportive as possible for you.

> If you have them available, use calming essential oils, like lavender or frankincense.

> Take other supportive measures for yourself if you can, like Bach Rescue Remedy, which is available from chemists.

> The best way to wash and turn the body for your safety. Check it is in the best position available in terms of bed height and access to both sides.

> Protection of the bed and whether waterproof protection is required.

Items You Will Need:

For dealing with body fluids, you will need absorbent bed and continence pads, wet wipes, and possibly also scissors—if they have a catheter—disposable gloves, bed protection, towels and waterproof dressings.

For washing the face and body, you will need face cloths, towels, a basin, soap or wet wipes, mouthwash, sponges, a toothbrush, a hairbrush or comb, Vaseline or lip salve, moisturising lotion and possibly also a new safety razor, shaving cream, denture fixative, dry shampoo cap and nail clippers or a file.

For ongoing care, you will need a strong bed sheet, cooling packs, a handkerchief or a cloth for their face, insect repellent and an insect net for open windows. You may wish to use essential oils for their antibacterial properties, as an insect repellent, for odour control and for a supportive atmosphere—see Appendix 2. You may also wish to use flowers and candles.

Protection of yourself from body fluids. Always be prepared for the unexpected release of fluid from the bladder, bowel, mouth and any open wounds. An apron and gloves are adequate protection in most circumstances. The infection risk is the same as when the person was alive, so use the same degree of protection.

Whether, and how, you wish to honour the person's body and your act of service. Whilst these are practical steps, you may wish to take time as you do them to connect with the person who has taken their last breath, regarding them still as a person. For instance, as you wash their mouth, you might thank them for all it has said.

Getting Started

If you want to do everything, this is the order of steps we recommend.

Lay flat on one pillow. Keep hands on top of the body as much as possible.

If the person took their last breath sitting up, we recommend lying them flat, initially, with one pillow under their head. Keep their hands on top of their body as much as possible to avoid discolouration.

Dealing with Body Fluids
You will need the following items:
- Soap, water and wash cloths. Wet wipes or cleansing foam may also be useful.
- Towels for drying and for covering exposed areas of the body.
- A continence pad or towel for under the pelvis.
- Scissors or a syringe if there is a catheter in place.

If someone has been ill before their last breath, they have usually been sleepy for several days and not eaten or drunk much, so there may not be much fluid in their body. However, it is prudent to be prepared for some urine in their bladder, faeces in their bowel and fluid in their stomach and lungs. Remember that when blood circulation stops, muscles relax. That includes the muscles which control our bladder and bowels. Anything in them is likely to come out naturally. After death, the body's structures change, so fluid can move around and will move to the lowest point because of gravity.

We recommend using continence pads with tabs, as they are absorbent and relatively easy to put on. Some people are uncomfortable using them because they are similar to nappies, so we want you to know that there are also alternatives to wear with pants. At the very least, we recommend placing a towel under the person's pelvis to absorb urine or faeces.

Turning someone right over onto their side will usually enable you to clean up any fluid likely to come from their mouth.

Here are the steps we would take:

1. With a continence pad or towel under their pelvis, press gently on their tummy to release urine.

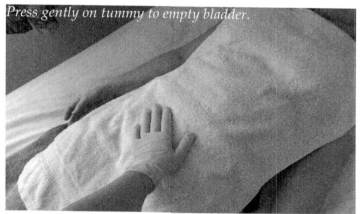
Press gently on tummy to empty bladder.

2. Place a towel or pad beside their face, on the side you will turn it towards.
3. Turn their body well over onto its side to check for faeces and to release fluid from their mouth.

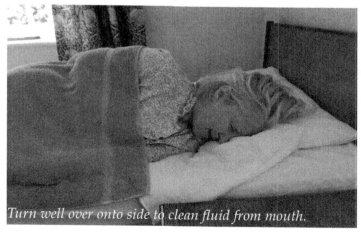
Turn well over onto side to clean fluid from mouth.

4. Clean soiled areas.
5. Secure a clean continence pad or towel over their back passage to absorb urine or faeces and then turn the person onto their back.

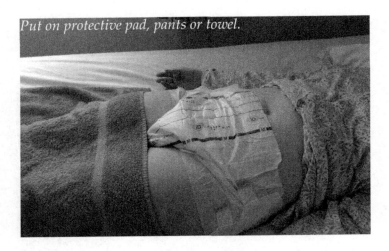
Put on protective pad, pants or towel.

6. Elevate the person's head with two pillows to control any further fluid seepage from their mouth.

Please note: If there is a urinary catheter, it is held in the bladder by a balloon filled with about two teaspoonfuls of water. To remove the catheter, either withdraw the water from the balloon with the syringe, or cut the tube with scissors, allowing the water to come out of the balloon. You can then gently pull the tube out of the body.

Cleaning Their Mouth
If you intend for someone to stay at home for several days, we would recommend paying attention to cleaning the mouth, as this can be a source of odour.

You will need the following items:
- Toothbrush, mouth sponge, cotton bud or a piece of gauze wrapped around a gloved finger.
- Glass of mouthwash or water with antibacterial essential oils such as lavender.
- Lip balm, Vaseline or oily cream.

1. Clean any fluid or mucus out of their mouth, replacing

the cleaning fluid several times if necessary.

2. Take your time to thoroughly clean their gums, tongue, teeth and back of the mouth.
3. Once clean, wipe over their mouth surfaces again with mouthwash on a small sponge. This helps to reduce odour and should be repeated regularly if necessary.
4. Gently smooth lip balm, Vaseline, oil or oily cream onto their lips to help prevent them from drying out.

Covering Wounds

Fluid may come from wounds on the lower body, such as pressure sores on the sacrum—the shield-shaped, bony structure at the base of the spine. Sometimes, people have fluid coming from areas of their skin before they die too. If someone has been nursed at home with wounds, then waterproof dressings are likely to be available, and the wounds may already be adequately dressed. Check for signs of fluid leaking and use dressings to cover the wound if necessary. It needs to be well sealed rather than neat. If you sense any odour coming from the wounds, then the dressings can be changed, and you can use essential oils to address the odour. Contact community nurses for advice and dressings if required. Alternatively, buy some from a chemist or supermarket.

Removing Pacemakers

For cremation, pacemakers must be removed. If you feel able to, it is possible to remove the pacemaker by making an incision in the skin where you can feel the pacemaker, taking out the device and cutting the wires. Then, place a dressing over the area. Otherwise, you can ask a doctor or funeral director to assist you. This can be done later.

Closing Their Eyes

Eyes often do not naturally close. They can be continually

open before someone's last breath if the person becomes too weak to keep them closed. It is usually only necessary to gently move the eyelid closed with a finger and hold it for a few seconds. Traditionally, an old penny—the size of a 2p piece—would have been placed on each eye to keep them closed.

Bear in mind that it is not always possible to close eyes fully. This is not a problem unless it is disturbing someone, in which case, find a handkerchief, scarf or small cloth to cover the face of the person who has taken their last breath. Alternatively, contact a funeral director who can insert spiked eye caps.

Try these steps:
1. Gently close the lids with the side of your finger and hold them closed for about 10 seconds.

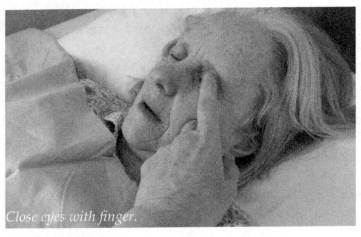
Close eyes with finger.

If this does not work, then try steps two or three.
2. Place a small bag of rice or an eye relaxation bag over the eyes for a couple of hours, or
3. Place a tiny piece of tissue or Vaseline under the eyelid.

Gently smoothing oil or oily cream onto the eyelids can help to stop them from drying out.

Replacing Dentures

Replacing dentures can feel challenging but is often important to people. Be aware that if the person is not wearing their dentures, they were probably removed because their gums have shrunk and they were uncomfortable.

If it is necessary to replace dentures, it needs to be done before their body becomes stiff. We recommend you do not try to do it without denture fixative.

1. Clean the mouth thoroughly as before.
2. Rinse the dentures in mouthwash or water with added antibacterial essential oil—lavender or tea tree.
3. Apply denture fixative generously to the dentures.
4. Insert the dentures into the mouth and press firmly into place.
5. Check the dentures are secure. If they are not, leave them out.

Closing Their Mouth

Bear in mind that it is not always possible to close the mouth fully. It is not a problem unless it is disturbing people. In this case, find a handkerchief, scarf or small cloth to cover the face. Alternatively, a funeral director can stitch or glue the mouth closed.

Try these steps first:

1. Place a pillow under the person's head to tilt it slightly forwards.
2. Place a rolled-up hand towel under their chin to gently push it upwards.
3. Keep this in place for at least 15 minutes or until the muscles stiffen due to rigor mortis.

Please note: We do not recommend tying a soft scarf or bandage under their chin and around the top of their head, as it can leave marks. If you do want to do this, however, smooth out creases where it touches their face.

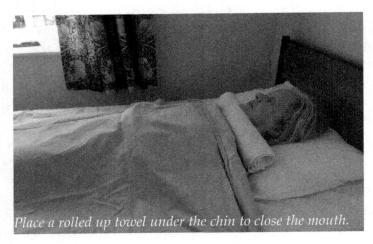

Place a rolled up towel under the chin to close the mouth.

Washing and Dressing

Washing and dressing the body can be an opportunity to take time to honour the person who has taken their last breath and to make a meaningful connection with them. It can be a remarkable expression of love if you wish it to be. Traditionally, washing this way would begin at the feet and move up the body to the head.

There is no right or wrong way to wash and dress the person who has taken their last breath—it may not even be necessary to wash them at all depending on people's views and wishes and when they were last washed. This is not much different from giving a bed bath to someone who is unconscious. It is easier if you have experience of this, or if someone who is helping does, as there are safe techniques for moving someone in bed.

Our main recommendation is to follow your instincts about what is needed. It is easier to wash and dress the body before or after rigor mortis while it is not stiff. If necessary, muscles can usually be massaged to move as required. You will not cause damage if you are gentle.

Here are a few tips:

If you want to wash someone, we recommend that you first consider their hair. If washing it is necessary, it is best to do this first, and we suggest using a dry shampoo. Place a towel under their head, dust on the powder and brush it out. Alternatively, use a dry shampoo cap, available from chemists. Be mindful of the person's usual hairstyle.

If you are shaving the face, use plenty of shaving oil or cream. Take care not to cause razor burn, as this can leave marks.
Consider cutting clothes to ease their removal.

If you have them, add antibacterial essential oils to the washing water. We like lavender, sage or rosemary but not tea tree for this because it often smells too strongly.

Consider massaging the skin with oil containing essential oils. Frankincense is a good option here—see Appendix 2.

Before dressing the person's body, consider cooling options, and place cool packs around their torso if that is your chosen option.

When redressing the person, consider cutting any clothes up the middle of the back to the collar, leaving the collar intact. This helps to place them more easily over the head and around the body.

Cooling the Body Using Cool Packs

You can use picnic-type ice blocks, physiotherapy-type gel packs or Cool Cubes—see Chapter 15.

1. Freeze the cool packs.
2. Wrap them individually, or in twos, in a pillowcase or towel to absorb condensation.
3. Place a block underneath each side of the body above the waist, to help to cool the kidneys, and place blocks on the tummy and chest areas.

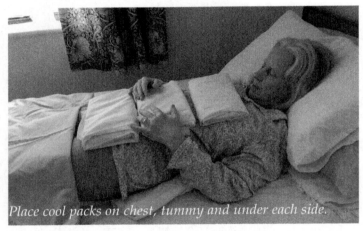

Place cool packs on chest, tummy and under each side.

4. Change the packs with frozen ones—two or three times on the first day—until the body has cooled.
5. Check the body daily to see if changes are required, and refresh packs as necessary. People often get into the routine of doing this every morning. If someone has been caring for the person, this is a task they may wish to undertake.

Raise the Head on a Pillow

After dressing and placing the cool packs—if you use them— keep the person's head raised and tilted slightly forwards, with an extra pillow if necessary. This helps to prevent any fluid from coming out of the mouth.

Tilt head forward with two pillows.

Controlling the Natural Transformation Processes
The main way of doing this is by cooling the body. As we have said, we recommend using cool packs, but you can also cool the room with an air conditioning unit if you prefer. It is possible to keep someone as cold as they would be in a mortuary fridge. Essential oils can also help.

Controlling Flies
We recommend taking steps to control flies. Flies are an essential part of nature's incredible process, which allows us all to live on this planet. They lay eggs that can turn into larvae within 48 hours. Whilst this is potentially a problem, it is not a big concern, as simple measures can prevent it:

Apply essential oils, like cedarwood, to the skin and use a diffuser in the room to neutralise any fly-attracting odour.
Advise people to be aware of flies entering the room.

Apply cedarwood essential oil or insect repellent around the person's body.

After the first day, tape an insect net over open windows. These can be purchased quite cheaply.

After the first day, keep windows and doors closed as much as possible when no one is present.

Cover the face with a cloth sprinkled with insect repellent when no one is present. Alternatively, pull a sheet up to cover the head.

Cover face when unattended.

Controlling Odour
Odour could come from either bacterial activity in the body or from fluids, like faeces, leaking from the body. This is rarely a problem, especially in people who have died after not eating and drinking for some time.

This risk can be minimised by the following attention:

Remove and clean up fluids from the body.

Thoroughly cleanse the mouth.

Ensure a continence pad is neatly fitted to absorb urine and faeces.

Apply essential oils, mixed in a carrier oil, to the skin—see Appendix 2.

Sprinkle 'Thieves Oil' around the body and perhaps use it in an oil diffuser. Note that flowery scents, like rose, can worsen any odour.

Keep the body cool.

Things To Remember
The most important thing to remember is to take one day at a time. It is natural to feel apprehensive the first few times you tend to someone after their last breath. Also, remember that you can change your mind at any time if it no longer feels right to have the person's body at home.

Important Things To Remember:

Make sure the atmosphere in the room is as comfortable and supportive as possible for you.

If you have them available, use calming essential oils like lavender or frankincense.

Take other supportive measures for yourself if you can—for example, Bach Rescue Remedy, which is available from chemists.

Expect gradual changes in the skin colour and appearance.

Remove warm bed clothes and cool the room and the person's body as soon as possible if they will be staying with you for a few days.
If you are using cooling packs, check and replace them daily.

You will know by the smell, just as when someone is alive, if there are body fluids requiring attention.

Keep flies out of the room as much as possible and keep the face covered when unattended.
If the person's face is disturbing someone, then cover it with a cloth.

Call for help if you have any concerns at all—either an organisation like Pushing Up the Daisies or a funeral director.

Authors

Lin Carruthers and Kate Clark

Lin's curiosity has taken her into the realms of engineering, art and writing. When she was in her thirties, the death of people her own age inspired her to learn about alternatives to traditional funerals and burials since she had found their funerals unhelpful. Coming from a hands-on, proactive family, she accepted it as normal to be involved in creating and speaking at funerals of people who were important to her, but the sense that something was missing remained. Then, she met Kate and learned about tending to someone after their last breath and looking after herself at the same time. She is currently a trustee of Pushing Up the Daisies and is delighted and honoured to be able to share, within this book, what she has learned.

Kate's first memory of death is being lifted up at the age of five to see her granny in her coffin. In her mid-thirties, her experiences of her beloved uncle dying at home led her to change course from engineering to nursing so that she could support people in their choice to die at home. With 20 years of nursing experience in the NHS and with Marie Curie, Kate now works privately with people who are dying and their families. Ten years after her profound experiences in the days after her aunty's death, Kate was moved to found Pushing Up the Daisies, in 2016. She is currently a trustee of the charity and runs the educational initiatives which she created.

Acknowledgements

We give our deep gratitude to all who have gone before to lay this path for us.

Thank you to everyone who has supported and encouraged us, with special thanks to those who have shared their precious and poignant stories: they have taught us so much and inspired our work over the years.

Thank you to Diana, Morag, Joanne, Ann, Rosemary, Sue, Freya, Jenny, Isabel, Deirdre, Susie, Jane, John and Charlotte for your generosity in sharing your inspiring stories for this book.

Thank you to the Pushing Up the Daisies 'After the Last Breath' course participants for your curiosity, questions and willingness to learn.

Thank you to Avigail Abarbanel for helping us to make sense of how our brains work.

Thank you to Fliss, Charlotte, Jane and Susan for guiding us through the editing and publication process so beautifully.

And thank you to everyone who has contributed in any way to the creation of this book. You know who you are.

Reviews

"From the opening pages, you know you are in safe hands that are guiding you with care and solid experience through the many possibilities, helping you to find the best way forwards for you and yours."

Rehana Rose, Director of Dead Good film.

"This book is a helpful and practical guide in a time that can be bewildering. Written compassionately, it gives options of what to do when a person close to you dies. It is well structured and full of practical information that can be easily found. I thoroughly enjoyed the moving, real-life experiences throughout this book."

Dietmar Hartmann, Retired Consultant Anaesthetist, NHS Tayside.

"A very comprehensive guide for anyone who is facing the uncertainty of someone dying. I can imagine lots of people finding it really helpful, and also soothing, to know they aren't alone in feeling confused, frightened or unsure of how to manage when someone dies. We're all in this together, and this very practical book reflects this beautifully."

Sue Brayne, Author of *Living Fully, Dying Consciously: The Path to Spiritual Wellbeing*.

"A gem of a book, chock-full of useful information and guidance. Lin and Kate guide us in exploring a variety of options and their key advice to us is 'slow down', to take our time after we lose a loved one. They share their own experiences of losing beloved family members and introduce us to a number of people exploring different options as they face death. In a society where death and dying have long been taboo, *Slow Down When Someone Dies* proves an honest and refreshing read."

Caroline Mackay, Celebrant.

"This engaging book provides a kind, non-judgemental exploration of the options for looking after your loved one at home after they have died. The authors' expert advice covers practicalities and also recognises the essential mystery of this often-hidden part of life."

Mark Hazelwood, Chief Executive for the Scottish Partnership for Palliative Care.

"*Slow Down When Someone Dies* is an absolutely wonderful book. It is a fully comprehensive guide to everything you need to know at this critical time; choices, special arrangements, legalities etc. The information is supported throughout by moving and personal stories. But this is not just a book about what to do for our loved ones, it is an invitation to think about our own mortality and what we might want for ourselves."

Maggie La Tourelle, Author of *The Gift of Alzheimer's*.

Pushing up the Daisies

Pushing Up the Daisies is a pioneering Scotland-wide charity. Our aim is for everyone in Scotland to understand their practical options when someone they know takes their last breath, how to look after themselves immediately after someone dies and to be able to spend time with the person at home, if that is their wish. The charity operates an advice line and offers well-received, inspiring and informative education to hospice staff, end-of-life companions, celebrants and the general public.

The charity's Daisy Chain of volunteers around Scotland helps people consider all their options, including the option to keep someone in the privacy and comfort of home after their last breath.

More information about the charity is available on the website: www.pushingupthedaisies.org.uk.

The charity provides practical assistance for people wishing to take charge of someone after their last breath in the Moray area. This service is being developed as a model for other regions.

Sign up on the website to keep in touch with the growing network of people across Scotland who are interested in this work, and check out the YouTube channel—Pushing Up the Daisies Scotland—for inspiring and informative videos.

For more information call 0300 102 4444
or contact admin@pushingupthedaisies.org.uk.
Pushing Up the Daisies SC046808

Printed in Great Britain
by Amazon

23359794R00137